5 minutes off the Motorways

or

A Break from the Motorways

by

Hugh Cantlie

Co-author of

5 minutes off the motorway

(1995)

Over 200 pubs, hotels, restaurants and places of interest which are about five minutes from a motorway junction.

Published by Cheviot Books

1st Edition Sep 2001 Reprint Jan 2002
2003 Edition Sep 2002
2004 Edition Oct 2003
2005 Edition Oct 2004

Copyright   © Hugh Cantlie
Illustrations   © Hugh Cantlie
Plans   © Paul Cantlie

Cheviot Books,
Belford Hall, Belford, Northumberland NE70 7EY
Website: www.cheviotbooks.com
Email: enquiries@cheviotbooks.co.uk
Tel: 01668 213 313 FAX: 01668 213 778

ISBN 0-9539920-3-9

Printed and bound by SGC Printing, Merthyr Tydfil, CF48 3TD

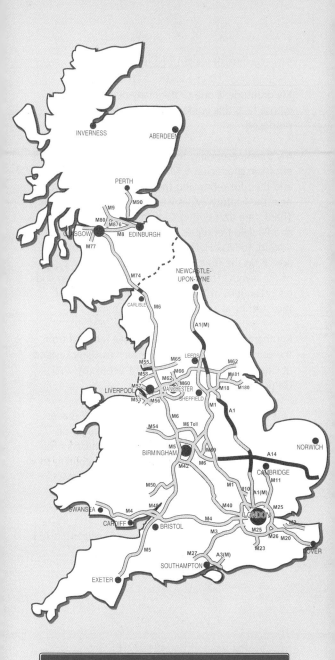

The Motorway Network

ACKNOWLEDGEMENTS

My gratitude is due to the many people without whose help this guide could not have been produced.

My thanks especially to my brother Paul for our joint efforts in producing 5 Minutes off the Motorway and then for redrawing the junction plans for Breaks near the Motorways as well as amending the maps. Thanks are also due to Cathering Hodson, Stephen and Pauline Henriques and many others for help in editing; to Max Herford and Toni Spowers for their advice on the front cover and Ned Hoste for design of the layout. Thanks are due to Mike Donovan and his colleagues at Stephens & George Limited for their technical assistance before printing.

My thanks also to all the help I have received from the publishing and book trade such as Daisy Leyland at Cheviot Books and the patient people at Gardners, Bertrams and Nielsens.

Last but not least I am grateful to all those readers who wrote in to suggest places which might be included or excluded. This made it much easier for me to check them out for myself before coming to a decision. The names of those people who have contributed to this edition are given separately. Please continue the good work!

Contents

Note from the Author

Dear Reader,

In my latest Guide I have tried to make taking a break from the Motorways less of a gamble! I have re-visited all the establishments listed and at the time of going to Press can recommend them all. I have based my recommendation on unannounced visits during which I looked not only at the standard of food and facilities but also the welcome, or not, afforded to children and dogs as well as caravans and horseboxes.

Entries are free of charge to the places mentioned as the guide is for the benefit of the motorist.

The Guide is intended to give you a clear idea of where and when to leave and re-join the Motorways and what you can expect when you arrive at the destination you have chosen. I have included places which are cheerful and comfortable and make a great alternative to the rigours of the service station. I have found they are better value for money.

This year I have also included the A14 which connects the Midlands to Felixstowe and now has numbered junctions.

Motorways where I could find nothing of merit are shown in the Index – one such motorway is the M8.

I am always pleased to have comments from my Readers so please use the listing sheets at the back of the Guide. If your suggestion is used in the next Edition you will be sent a free copy.

Enjoy your journey!

Hugh Cantlie

How to use you guide

Motorway Maps and Plans
The layout is relatively easy to follow. The motorways are in numerical order with a separate section for Scotland. Each map is orientated with north at the top. The scale depends on what has to be shown and how to fit it on to the page. The longer motorways have been divided up into sections.

Those junctions with places off them are shown with the appropriate junction number, whilst those with nothing to get off for are shown grey. This may help you work out the distances involved between likely stops.

Junctions
In the blue panel the junction number is given, followed by the towns and road numbers. There is then a short introduction of any difficulties you may find (from personal experience) together with a plan, showing filling stations and the entries. Places of interest nearby are given.

Places of Interest
The names of historic houses or places of interest nearby are given with the initials in brackets of the owners where known. Those houses owned by members of the Historic Houses Association need to be contacted beforehand.

(EH)	*English Heritage.*
(HHA)	*Historic Houses Association.*
(HS)	*Historic Scotland.*
(NT)	*National Trust.*
(NTS)	*National Trust for Scotland.*

Description & Symbols

A brief description is given for each entry and includes attitudes to dogs and children; times for the last orders for food as opposed to drinks and the number of bedrooms where applicable. The price range is indicated by the number of pound signs and a drawing gives an idea of what the place looks like to help recognition upon arrival.

Ⓐ	Location of entry
F/S	Filling station
🛏	Bedrooms available
♠	Breakfast for passing motorists
£	Price Bracket
✶	Particular Character

Prices

We have tried to give an indication of the price range based on the cost of an 8oz sirloin steak. These are as follows:

Under £9	£
£9-£11	££
£12-15	£££
Over £15	££££

The first two categories could be classified as good Pub food.

Accommodation prices vary but seem to be in line with the price of food. The beds have not been individually tested.

Readers Contributions

Additions

A1

17-34	Blue Cow	Peter Hopley
38-44	Green Man	John Stephens
48	Royal Oak	J. W. Newton

M1

19	Manor Farm Shop	James Grindal
29	Hardwick Inn	Jo Nicholson

M4

37	The Angel	Michael Knowles

M5

25	Hankridge Arms	Richard Mulligan

M6

19	Fryers Nurseries	Juliet Amery
35	New Inn	Stephen Henriques

M11

10	Tickell Arms	Angus Euren

M25

9	Leg of Mutton & Cauliflower	M. G. Briscoe

M50

3	Frederiques	Carolyn de Salis

M74

15	Moffat	Marilyn Elliott

A14

		Pat Andrews

Deletions

A1(M)

37	Marr Lodge	Tim O'Connor-Fenton

M62

37	Wellington Arms	Liz Pringle

A1(M)

London to Newcastle

Junctions 6 to 63

The A1 was the old Great North Road between London and Edinburgh. The building of the M1 and the M6 reduced its importance but with the level of traffic rising efforts were and are being made to upgrade it to motorway standard.

At the moment only six sections have been so modernised but the numbering of the junctions is on the basis that they will all be linked up eventually.

These sections are: the southern part from the M25 to Baldock, the Peterborough section, the Doncaster part, the junction with the M1, the Boroughbridge section and lastly the part from Scotch Corner to Newcastle.

SOUTHERN SECTION 6 to 10

A boring stretch getting out of London.

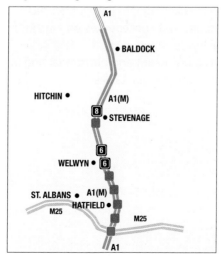

| 6 | Welwyn Garden City A1000 |

A complicated system of roundabouts, but worth the effort as Welwyn (as opposed to Welwyn Garden City) is a pleasant market town to this day.

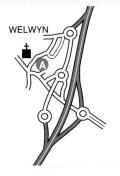

WELWYN

Places of interest
The Roman Baths. George Bernard Shaw's house at Ayot St Lawrence – 3m

 ## The White Hart
Welwyn
☎ 01438 715 353
Last orders: 2.00pm. Lunches only. Closed on Sundays.
££

Once a coaching inn, it no longer has bedrooms but concentrates on lunches for local businessmen.
It has a restaurant and bar specialising in roast beef and fresh vegetables.

London to Newcastle

8 · Hitchin
Stevenage (N) A602

Stevenage was once a sleepy country town and then became one of the first New Towns in the 1950s. There is little reason to go through it, unless to visit Knebworth House, for which Junction 7 is closest. The village of Little Wymondley is attractive in rather a chintzy way but nevertheless pleasant. Graveley on the Old Great North Road has changed little.

Ⓐ The Bucks Head
Little Wymondley
☎ 01438 353 320
Last orders: 2.15pm and 9.30pm
9.00pm on Sundays.
£

It has been an inn for some 400 years. It is a locals' pub without frills but with a children's playground, a family room, outside seating, a car park and Petanque. Children and dogs are welcome.

8 Hitchin
Stevenage (N) A602

B **The Waggon and Horses**
Graveley
☎ 01438 367 658
Last orders: 2.30pm and 9.00pm,
No evening meals on Sundays.
£

It was most probably a coaching
stop but is now a tenanted
pub serving bar meals, coffees
and teas. It has a beer garden
overlooking the village
pond and a car park.
Children welcome.

C **Plume of Feathers**
Little Wymondley
☎ 01438 729 503
Last orders: 2.00pm and 9.15pm.
No evening meals on Fridays and Sundays.
££

A small 18th Century house with an inglenook
fireplace which has been made into a homily
pub, with a restaurant and a bar, a patio
and outside seating.
Children and dogs on leads
are welcome.

London to Newcastle

PETERBORO' SECTION 13 to 17

The most recent part of the A1(M) to be built to motorway standards. It is unusual in having four lanes which could be a sign of future growth in traffic.

Not the most attractive part of England but Huntingdon is Cromwell country and there are some interesting places, such as Buckden Palace and Island Hall. To the north it continues past Grantham and Newark to Blyth as a dual carriageway. There are several well known hostelries where you can stop such as the The Ram Jam near Oakham and The Blue Cow Inn in South Witham.

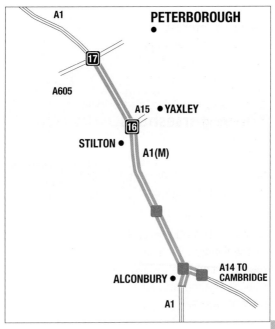

16 Yaxley A15
Stilton (B1043)

The junction is easy, but finding the way through Yaxley is more difficult. Head for the steeple of the

church as a landmark and then left at the T junction beyond. The Three Horseshoes is along the village street on the right.

No difficulty to find the Bell Inn in Stilton.

Places of interest
Peterborough Cathedral – 4m.
Elton Hall (HHA) – 5m
Southwick Hall (HHA)

Three Horseshoes
Yaxley
☎ 01733 242 059
Last orders: 2.00pm and 9.00pm.
9.30pm on Fridays and Saturdays.
££

A cosy pub on the main street of the village which serves bar meals. A children's playground, outside seating and a car park at the rear.

16	Yaxley A15 Stilton (B1043)

B Bell Inn Hotel *
Stilton
☎ 01733 241 066
Last orders: 2.00pm and 9.30pm.
2.00pm and 9.30pm Sundays.
£££ 🛏

A 16th century coaching inn and now a privately owned well furnished hotel with 19 bedrooms, two bars and a restaurant on two levels under beamed ceilings.
There is outside seating in an enclosed garden and private parking.
Dick Turpin's room where he rested between operations is still in use as the resident's lounge.
Those looking for Stilton cheese will be disappointed as it was made in Melton Mowbray and sold here on the old coaching road.
The place is haunted so dogs are not welcome.

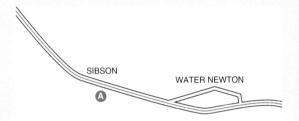

17 Peterborough
Oundle A605

The Sibson Inn is about 3 miles north of Junction 17, directly on the A1 to the left. Coming from the north, go past it and turn round on the crossing to Water Newton.

SIBSON

WATER NEWTON

Ⓐ

 The Sibson Inn
Stibbington
☎ 01780 782 227
Last orders:

££ 🛏 🍷

A friendly wayside inn, which was once a farm. It has recently changed hands and is being renovated. There are nineteen bedrooms in the converted outbuildings. Meals are served in the bar area and in the restaurant.

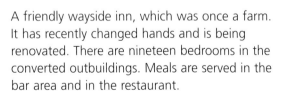

London to Newcastle

DONCASTER SECTION 34 to 38

One of the original sections to be rebuilt as a motorway. It intersects with the M18 linking the M1 to the M62.

South of Blyth it is dual carriageway all the way to Peterborough, but there are some well known places such as the Ram Jam Inn and the Blue Cow in South Witham. Past junction 38 on the way north there is a small edifice in fine ashlar stone on the right. This is Robin Hood's Well which was designed by Sir John Vanbrugh for the 3rd Earl of Carlisle.

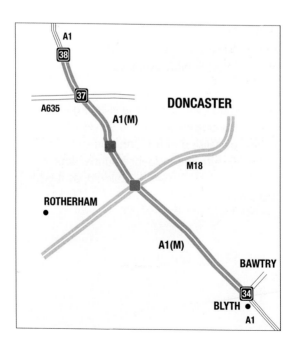

34   Bawtry A614
Worksop B6045

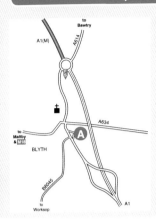

An easy junction but for those driving up from the south, it is best to get off onto the slip road a mile or so beforehand which is signed Maltby A634.

White Swan
Blyth
☎ 01909 591 222
Last orders: 2.00pm and 9.30pm.
No meals on Sunday evenings.
££

A small pub overlooking the village green with some outside seating. It serves bar meals specialising in fish and home made dishes. Due to the resident hounds, dogs are discouraged as well as children, as it is too small to cope.

> ### 37 Doncaster A635
> Barnsley

A straightforward junction posing no problems. A filling station just beyond the turning.

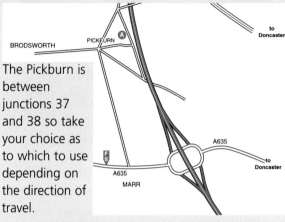

BRODSWORTH   PICKBURN   to Doncaster

The Pickburn is between junctions 37 and 38 so take your choice as to which to use depending on the direction of travel.

A635   to Doncaster

A635
MARR

Places of interest
Brodsworth Hall (EH) – 3m

Ⓐ Pickburn Arms
Nr Brodsworth
☎ 01302 721 656
Last orders: 2.00pm and 9.00pm.
No meals on Sunday evenings.
££

A modern pub owned by Avebury Taverns, it is nevertheless a friendly place laod out in a series of eating areas and carveries. There is a large garden at the rear with outside seating and a childrens play area. An equally large car park for horse boxes and caravans. Children welcomed but dogs outside.

A1(M)

London to Newcastle

BORO'BRIDGE SECTION 44 to 49

This section is in two parts, both of recent construction. The short southern section is the junction with the M1 extension. From Junction 45 it is a dual carriageway until Junction 46, skirting past Wetherby. At Junction 49 a decision has to be taken whether to continue on the A1 to Scotch Corner or head for the Tyne Tunnel near Newcastle on the A19 past Middlesborough.

Boroughbridge is a pleasant market town.

The motorway south of Junction 45 is being extended and is due to open in spring 2005, but is not included in this edition.

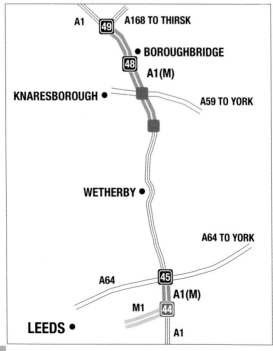

44	Sherburn B1227
	Selby A63

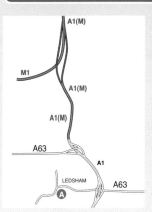

Ledsham is 3 miles south of the M1 and A1(M) interchange. It is surprisingly easy to find as there are feeder roads coming off the A1(M) in both directions

Ⓐ Chequers Inn   *

Ledsham
☎ 01977 683 135
Last Orders 2.15 and 9.15pm. From 11am on Saturdays. Closed all day Sunday
£££

A Free House in the middle of this Estate village. The reason why it is closed all day on Sunday is because the lady of the manor in 1830 was abused on her way to church by estate workers pouring out of the pub. Bar meals downstairs and a comfortable restaurant above. The two chefs cook to order from an imaginative menu. Well behaved children and dogs are welcome.

45 York A64
Leeds

For those going to Bramham on the dual carriageway, come off the A1 and follow the signs to Bramham. The Hazelwood Castle Hotel is brown signed on the road

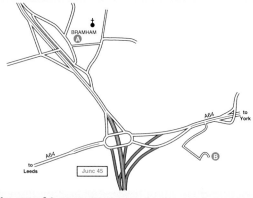

Places of interest
Bramham Park. (HHA) ½ mile

Ⓐ The Red Lion
Bramham
☎ 01937 843 524
Last orders: 2.00pm and 8.45pm.
No evening meals on Sunday.
££

A simple village pub, which has been extended by annexing the butcher's shop next door as a restaurant. A cheerful place with attentive service.
A beer garden and car park. Children and dogs welcome.

| 45 | York A64 |
| --- | Leeds |

Ⓑ Hazlewood Castle Hotel
Hazlewood
☎ 01937 535 353
Last orders: 9.30pm in the restaurant (which does not serve lunches except on Sundays) From 11.00am to 9.30pm in the Pizzeria.
££££

An imposing castle set in 77 acres of grounds. Listed in the Domesday Book it was crenellated in 1290. It has now been converted into a privately owned hotel with 21 bedrooms. Previously it was occupied by Carmelite monks, who would have had a simpler life style than that now offered. These include the 1086 Restaurant, conference and banqueting suites, musical events and clay pigeon shoots. For those in more of a rush there is the Prickly Pear Pizzeria.

48 Ripon Dishforth (A168)
Boroughbridge A6055

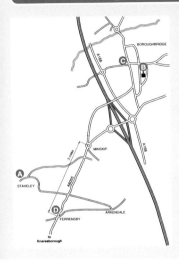

Boroughbridge was a coaching stop on the Great North Road and has some interesting places.

Places of interest
Roman town of Isurium.

Royal Oak
Staveley
☎ 01423 340 267
Last orders: 1.45pm and 8.45pm. 8.00pm on Sundays. No food on Mondays.
£££

A Free House in a rural village. A congenial atmosphere, even after you have walked out having forgotten to pay the bill! Eating areas as opposed to a restaurant. Outside seating and a beer garden. Parking for horseboxes. Children and dogs welcome but dogs outside. It is brown signed from Minskip.

48 Ripon Dishforth (A168)
Boroughbridge A6055

B ## The Dining Room
Boroughbridge
☎ 01423 326 426
Last orders: 9.30pm on Weekdays - No
lunches including Saturdays. 2pm for lunch
only on Sundays. Closed all day Mondays.
£££

A family owned restaurant in the centre of
the town. It is small and comfortable
with an imaginative
menu. Well behaved
children but no dogs
allowed.
Advisable to
reserve.

C ## Rose Manor Hotel
Boroughbridge
☎ 01423 322 245
Last orders: 2.00pm and 9.00pm.
9pm on Sundays.
£££   🛏

A privately owned hotel in its
own grounds with 20
bedrooms and a
restaurant.
It is well known for
its excellent afternoon
teas. Children
welcome.

48 Ripon Dishforth (A168)
Boroughbridge A6055

Ⓓ General Tarleton *

Ferrensby

☎ 01423 340 284

Last orders: 2.15pm and 9.30pm

8.30pm on Sundays.

£££ 🛏

A privately owned restaurant and hotel with 14
bedrooms. It is reputed to have the best cuisine
in Yorkshire with a warm welcome from a
young professional staff in a relaxed
atmosphere. Dogs and children welcome
provided they behave.

49	Thirsk A168 Teeside (A19)

For the Crab and Lobster, you can get off the A168 and return to the A1 easily enough, provided you follow the plan.

The Nags Head is some 8 miles north of Junction 49 so only just within reach. There is a turning to the east off a gap in the carriageway to Pickhill.

The A1 continues as a dual carriageway to Scotch Corner where it becomes a Motorway again. There are some excellent places just off the A1 such as the Green Man in Exelby.

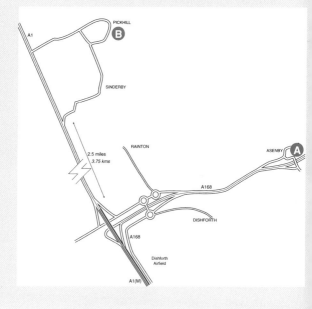

49   Thirsk A168
Teeside (A19)

Ⓐ The Crab and Lobster ∗
Asenby
☎ 01845 577 286
Last orders: 2.15pm and 9.15 pm
2.00pm and 9.00 pm on Sundays.
££££ 🛏

One of the best places for a stopover on a
motorway! The decor has been done with flair
and the set menu (which obviously specialises
in fish) is value for money.
The Crab Manor Hotel next door
is in the same ownership
and has 11 bedrooms
with an eclectic mix
of furniture and styles.

Ⓑ Nags Head ∗
Pickhill
☎ 01845 567 391
Last orders: 2.00pm and 9.30 pm
£££ 🛏

It is really a restaurant in an agricultural village
with a separate dining room and bar meals at
well appointed bar. A good wine list. Much
frequented by the surrounding folk. There are
16 bedrooms.
Children and
dogs allowed
with well
behaved
owners.

London to Newcastle

NEWCASTLE SECTION 56 to 63

The most northerly section built to motorway standards so far. It starts at Scotch Corner and ends south of Gateshead with a spur leading towards the Tyne Tunnel. South of Scotch Corner it is dual carriageway to Junction 49 south of Boroughbridge. The Green Man in Exelby is a good place to stop.

This stretch is not very interesting but Durham Cathedral "the loveliest building on Planet Earth" is just off the motorway and the Angel of the North will greet you at the other end.

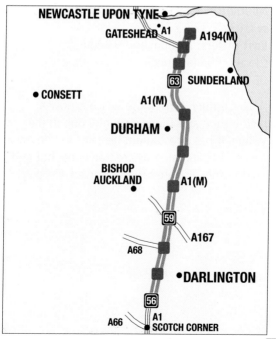

56 Pierce Bridge B6275
Bishop Auckland B6275

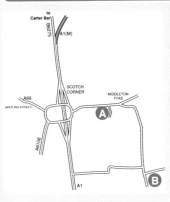

There are no places near this junction, but two miles to the south is the junction with the A66 known as Scotch Corner, where there are two excellent stop overs.

Ⓐ The Shoulder of Mutton ∗
Middleton Tyas
☎ 01325 377 271
Last orders: 2.00pm and 9.30pm.
Closed Monday Lunch.
££

A 16 Century farmhouse which is now a picturesque and friendly country pub in the village. It has a restaurant upstairs and below a beamed ceiling area where traditional hot and cold freshly prepared food is served. No dogs.

56 Pierce Bridge B6275
Bishop Auckland B6275

ⒷThe Black Bull ✳

Moulton
☎ 01325 377 289
Last orders: 2.00pm and 10.00pm.
Closed Sundays.
££££

One of the best known places in this part of Yorkshire and privately owned. It has a conservatory restaurant as well as several dining areas and a bar which serves bar meals. In addition there is Hazel - a Pullman carriage from the Brighton Belle- which is used for dinners. No children under 7. It is advisable to book.

59 Newton Aycliffe A167
Darlington A167

The Foresters Arms is on the left at the end of the stretch of dual carriageway.

To get to The County, skirt past the roundabout and just beyond the church turn right at the traffic lights. Ignore the pub which is on the bend facing you but turn right again onto the village green. The County is immediately to the left.

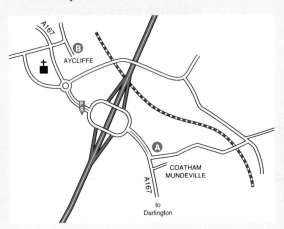

| 59 | Newton Aycliffe A167 |
| | Darlington A167 |

A Foresters Arms
Coatham Mundeville
☎ 01325 320 565
Last Orders 3.00pm and 9.45pm.
Closed Sunday evenings.
£

A simple country pub but with a small restaurant and bars. Outside there is a children's playground and seating when the sun shines. Dogs are however not welcome.

B The County
Aycliffe Village
☎ 01325 312 273
Last Orders 2.00pm and 9.30pm
No evening meals on Sundays.
£££

A renovated country style pub on the village green. Its was brought to public notice as Tony Blair brought President Chirac of France to have dinner here.
Restricted outside seating.
Children are suffered but no dogs.
French not essential.

63 Chester Le Street A167
Stanley A693

An easy junction to start with as Lumley Castle is signed. Then the signs disappear but keep bearing left and they will reappear.

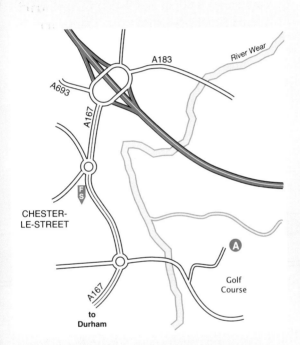

Places of interest

St Peter's Church in Chester-le-Street (where St Cuthbert's body rested for a 100 years before final burial at Durham Cathedral).
Beamish Open Air Museum.

63 Chester Le Street A167
Stanley A693

 Lumley Castle ＊

Chester Le Street

☎ 0191 389 1111

Last orders: 2.00pm and 9.30pm.
No lunches on Saturdays.

££££ ⊨

Built in 1389 by Sir Ralph Lumley it is still
owned by the family. For the past 25
years it has been leased out as a friendly,
efficient and comfortable hotel with 59
bedrooms. The Great Hall is still used for
its original purpose to welcome guests for
a meal but there are two other excellent
restaurants and a bar serving sandwiches.
It is surrounded by 9 acres of garden and
over the road there is a golf course.
Although the bedrooms are all plumbed,
the roof structures and massive walls
prevent the installation of lifts. Children
but no dogs.

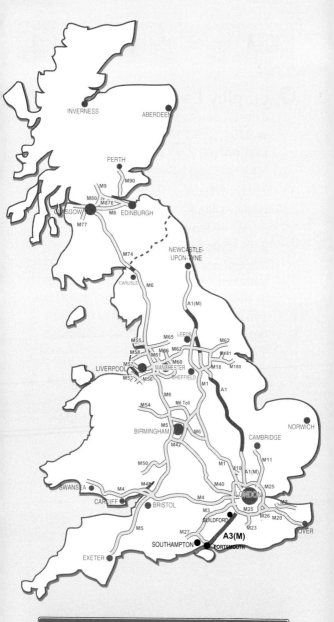

A3(M)

Horndean to Portsmouth

A short stretch of motorway, completed in 1979, to ease the junction of the A3 to the M27.

Coming from the north after Petersfield it passes Butser Celtic Farm before climbing up to the high ground overlooking Portsmouth, the naval dockyards and the broad expanse of Portsmouth harbour, once full of warships. Along the heights are a string of fortifications built by Palmerston in the1860s to protect the coast from an invasion by the French.

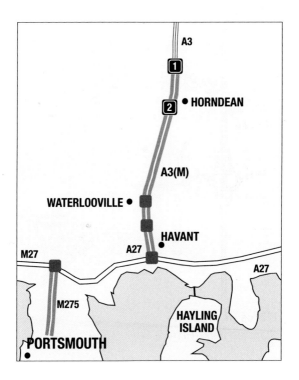

2 Horndean
Cowplain B2149

Coming from the north take the slip road to Horndean.

Get on again at Junction 2 further south. It could be a little complicated.

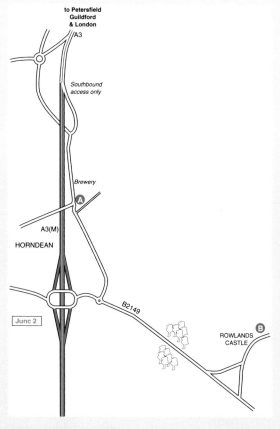

Places of interest
Stansted Park (HHA) – 5m

2 Horndean
Cowplain B2149

A The Ship and Bell Hotel.
Horndean
☎ 02392 592 107
Last orders: 2.30pm and 9.30pm.
No evening meals on Sundays.
ff 🛏

It has been a coaching inn since 1671 and
was probably the last stop for Nelson's
officers before joining their ships. It has
14 bedrooms, a restaurant, two bars and
serves home cooked fare. A traditional
old English hotel,
which has seen
kinder days.

B The Robin Hood *
Rowlands Castle
☎ 02392 412 268
Last orders: 2.00pm and 9.00pm.
fff

It has opened as a restaurant and is just
within five minutes from the junction. A
friendly atmosphere, light and airy,
looking out over the village green.
Outside seating where children and dogs
are welcome.

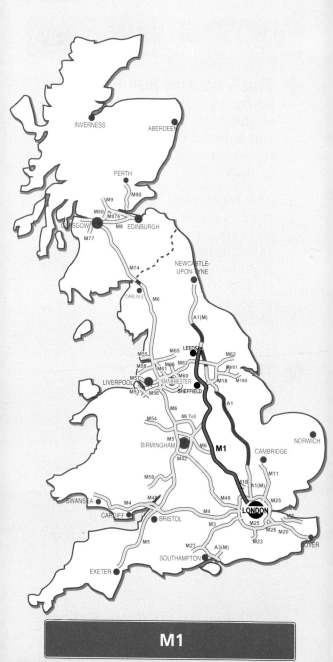

M1

London to Leeds

Junctions   6   to   47

The M1 was the first major motorway to be built in the U.K. The first section of 72 miles was built by Messrs Laing & Son at a cost of £50 million and was completed in 19 months. It was opened in November 1959 by the then Minister of Transport, Ernest Marples, who in real life was a director of a building contracting firm. On the day of the opening an elderly woman crashed her fast Mercedes sports car which resulted in the immediate imposition of speeding restrictions. The final link of the M1, from Leeds to the A1(M) of about 9 miles, was completed in 1999 at a cost of £190 million.

SOUTHERN SECTION   9   to   18

A congested section of the motorway until past the junction with the M6.

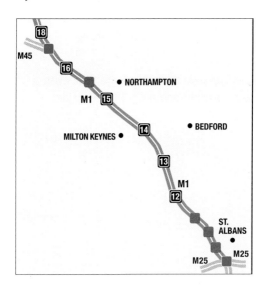

12 Woburn   Houghton Regis
        Flitwick A5120

Toddington is an attractive village with a large
green. There are several other pubs in addition to
those mentioned. Harlington is harder to find as it
is signposted only as Harlington Station.

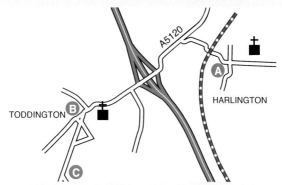

Ⓐ **The Carpenters Arms**
Harlington
☎ 01525 872 384
Last orders: 2.00pm and 9.00pm. No food on
Sunday evenings. Closed Mondays.
££

A cheerful low beamed village pub, with a beer
garden outside and a pool table inside.

B The Bell
Toddington
☎ 01525 872 564
Last orders: 3.00pm and 10.00pm.
No evening meals on Friday, Saturday
and Sunday.
££

It is a popular village pub overlooking the
green with small areas for eating and a bar.
Home cooking and a
cheerful atmosphere.
Outside seating and a
car park at the rear.
Children welcome.

C The Angel
Toddington
☎ 01525 872 380
Last orders: 2.00pm and 10.00pm.
9.00pm on Sundays
££

Reputed to date from the 16th century it is a
tenanted pub of Greene King Brewery. Bar
snacks are available, as is morning coffee.
There is a beer
garden. Disabled
facilities. Dogs
allowed outside.

13 Milton Keynes (S) Bedford A421 Ampthill A507   Woburn

The A4102 to Woburn passes through pleasant countryside. Aspley Guise is an attractive village.

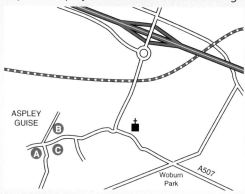

Places of interest
Woburn Abbey (HHA) – 2m
Bletchley Park – 8m

 # Moore Place Hotel
Aspley Guise
☎ 01908 282 000
Last orders: 1.45pm and 9.30pm. No lunch on Saturdays.
£££   🛏   🍸

A privately owned hotel, once a Georgian house built in 1786. It has 64 bedrooms mostly in two modern annexes, as well as The Greenhouse Restaurant and a bar. Children and dogs welcomed. Facilities for the disabled.

13 Milton Keynes (S) Bedford A421 Ampthill A507 Woburn

B The Anchor
Aspley Guise
☎ 01908 582 177
Last orders: 2.00pm and 9.00pm.
Closed Sunday evenings.
££

It has been a pub for more than 100 years and is owned by the brewery group Charles Wells. It serves coffee and bar meals. Children, dogs and coaches are all welcome.

C Aspleys Bar & Restaurant
Aspley Guise
☎ 01908 282 877
Last orders: 9.30pm. 10.00pm on Fridays and Saturdays. Closed on Sundays and Bank Holidays.
£££

Built in 1837 as a coaching inn and called the Bell. It is now a restaurant specialising in Italian food. Garden and car park at rear.

14　Milton Keynes
Newport Pagnell A509

A nondescript junction in open countryside.

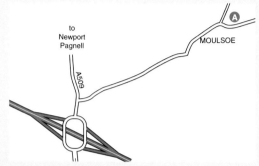

Places of interest
Bletchley Park – 6m
Chicheley Hall (HHA) – 3m

Ⓐ Carrington Arms ✳
Moulsoe
☎ 01908 218 050
Last orders: 2.30pm and 10.00pm.
9.30pm on Sundays
££££ 🛏

It is now part of a small group of independent
inns. Guests choose from a selection of prime
cuts of Scottish steak, fresh fish and seafood. It
is then cooked to their instructions on the
charcoal grill and served by a young attentive
staff. Bar snacks in the summer.
There are 8 bedrooms in
the modern stable block
to the rear. Dogs in the
garden but children
welcome.

15 Wellingborough (A45)
Northampton (S&E) A508

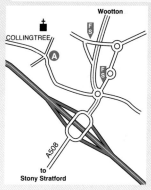

This junction has been altered recently to give access to a large industrial estate. However it is worth persevering as Collingtree is an attractive village.

Places of interest
Waterways Museum – 3m
Stoke Park Pavilions – 4m

A The Wooden Walls of Old England
Collingtree
☎ 01604 762 427
Last orders: 2.00pm and 9.00pm.
No lunches on Mondays.
£

The name stems from the old beams inside. A pleasant and cheerful atmosphere with log fires, serving Real Ales and bar meals. A children's playground and a family room. Dogs allowed outside. A car park and beer garden behind.

16   Daventry A45
Northampton A45

At the junction take the A45 to Daventry. After about two miles is the village of Flore. The Royal Oak is on the left

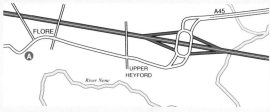

Places of interest
Althorp Hall (HHA) – 7m

 The Royal Oak
Flore
☎ 01327 341 340
Last orders: 3.00pm and 9.00pm. No evening meals on Sundays and no meals on Tuesdays.
££

An old fashioned pub selling Real Ales to real people.
It serves bar meals but there is a small restaurant area.
A large beer garden and a children's playground, so children and dogs are welcome.

> **18** Rugby Hinckley A5
> Daventry A428

Pay no attention to the large industrial park to the west but head towards Crick which is a pleasant village.

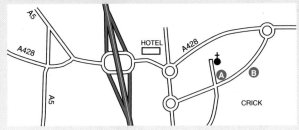

 The Wheatsheaf
Crick
☎ 01788 822 284
Last orders: 2.30pm and 9.00pm.
8.00pm on Sundays.
££

Records date the building to before 1620, but it has been known as the Wheatsheaf since 1742. It has been modernised to have a restaurant. A bar with a beer garden. Dogs allowed but only outdoors.

18 Rugby Hinckley A5
Daventry A428

Ⓑ **The Red Lion**
Crick
☎ 01788 822 342
Last orders: 2.00pm and 9.00pm.
ff

It has been a coaching inn since the early
1700s and is now family run.
It is low beamed, as tall visitors will discover.
Some outside seating and a car park at the
rear. A congenial place where they pride
themselves on their homemade steak pie
served with real ales. Morning coffee available.
Dogs welcome but children at lunch only.

MIDDLE SECTION 19 to 29

This seems to be a culinary desert with no oasis of peace.

However there are some interesting places to see off the motorway, such as Stanford Hall and the Civil War battlefield of Naseby off Junction 19. At Junction 27 is Lord Byron's old home of Newstead Abbey which he sold in 1816 when he went abroad. Lastly there are those stupendous buildings of Hardwicke Hall, Bolsover Castle, Sutton Scarsdale and further afield, Haddon Hall and Chatsworth.

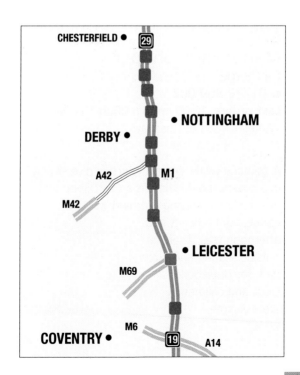

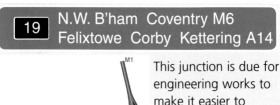

19 N.W. B'ham Coventry M6
Felixtowe Corby Kettering A14

This junction is due for engineering works to make it easier to interchange between the M1, M6 and A14

Places of interest
Stanford Hall

Ⓐ Manor Farm Shop *

Catthorpe

☎ 01788 869 002

Last orders: 10.00am to 6.00pm. 5.00pm in Winter. Closed on Tuesdays.

£

A genuine working farm which is diversifying. In a coverted barn there is a Craft Shop and the Tea Room serving morning coffee, light lunches and afternoon teas. There is outside seating and a car park for Horseboxes. Dogs and children are welcome.

29 Chesterfield A617
Matlock (A632)

This junction is studded with the brown signs of the Tourist Board. The sign to Heath can be missed, which is on the way to the gaunt ruins of Sutton Scarsdale.

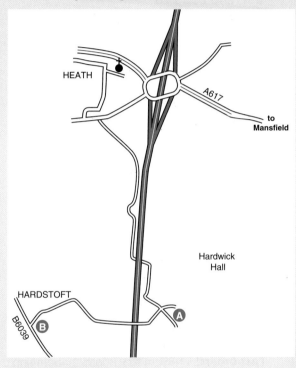

Places of interest
Hardwick Hall (NT) – 2m; Sutton Scarsdale (EH) – 1m; Chatsworth (HHA) – 15m; Haddon Hall (HHA) – 17m

29   Chesterfield A619
Matlock (A632)

Ⓐ The Weeping Ash
Hardstoff
☎ 01246 850 276
Last orders: 2.30pm and 9.30pm. No evening meals on Sundays. Closed Mondays
££

Part of a complex of barn conversions, it is a cheerful pub with an imaginative menu including ostrich steak. The bar snacks are more than generous and the beer is good. There are seven B&B bedrooms. Outside seating and a car park for horseboxes. Dogs and children allowed.

Ⓑ The Hardwick Inn
Hardwick Park
☎ 01246 850 245
Last orders: 11.30pm to 9.30pm. 1.45pm and 9.00pm on Sundays. Bar meals only on Mondays.
££ 🛏

A popular inn in a house built in the 17th Century. It has a range of eating areas and a restaurant. Plenty of outside seating and parking for cars and horse boxes. Children and dogs allowed, but dogs outside. It could become crowded during the summer.

London to Leeds

NORTHERN SECTION 30 to 48

Certainly not scenic but interesting as you drive through the industrial heartland of this part of England. There are places however to see on the way. These include the Cannon Hall Museum off Junction 37 and near Junction 46 there are Harewood House and Temple Newsam House known as the Hampton Court of the North.

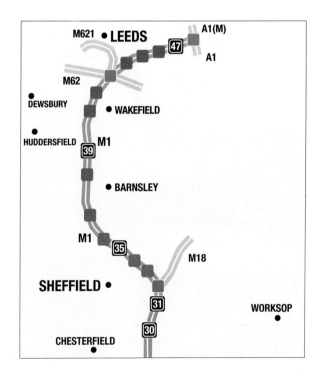

30   Sheffield A6135   Worksop A619
Chesterfield A619   Newark A616

Take the road to the left after the motorway and
drive down into the valley. Through the village and
the Sitwell Arms will be on the right.

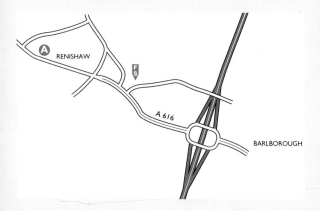

Places of interest

Renishaw Hall (HHA)
Barlborough Hall

30 Sheffield A6135 Worksop A619
Chesterfield A619 Newark A616

 The Sitwell Arms
Renishaw
☎ 01246 435 226
Last orders: 2.45pm and 9.45pm in the
restaurant. 2.00pm and 9.30pm in the
lounge bar.
££

A privately run hotel with 29 bedrooms, a
comfortable restaurant and two bars. There
is a garden and orchard and a car park in
front. They do have conferences and
weddings but these will not interfere with
the needs of passing motorists. Children
welcome and dogs by arrangement.

31 Sheffield Worksop A57

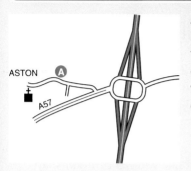

A simple junction but look out for the road to Aston cum Aughton, when you come off.

Ⓐ The Yellow Lion
Aston cum Aughton
☎ 01142 872 283
Last orders: 12.00pm and 9.00pm.
£

A simple locals' pub with stone flagged floors in a fairly built up area, but it overlooks fields. It serves home cooked bar meals and has a children's playground, family room and a beer garden. Dogs allowed. One Armed Bandits and a Pool Table.

35 Rotherham A629

An easy junction and one turns right almost immediately, as signed.

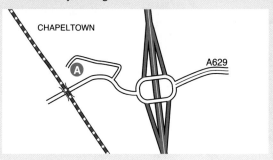

The Travellers
Thorpe Hesley
☎ 01142 467 870
Last orders: 2.30pm and 8.30pm.
No evening meals on Sunday and Monday evenings.
£

A surprise, as it is deep in a wood just off the motorway. It has recently been repainted and has a large beer garden at the rear with a childrens playground. Bar meals only served. Children and dogs welcome. An outside WC.

39 Wakefield A636
Denby Dale A636

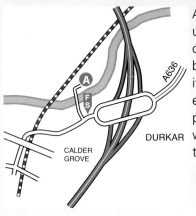

A fairly unimpressive part of the country, but redolent of its industrial past, especially the part played by waterborne transport.

Ⓐ The Navigation
Caldergrove
☎ 01924 274 361
Last orders: From noon to 8.00pm.
£

It is situated on the banks of the Calder and Heble Navigation. A simple pub now owned by Punch Pub Co, it was once the Dock Masters house, and judging from the photographs on the walls, an inn for boatmen. It serves bar meals and there is a large beer garden and play area on the banks of the canal, where children and dogs are welcome.

47 Garforth A642 The South A1 Castleford A656

The last junction on the M1 before it merges with a short section of the new A1 Motorway. Aberford is an attractive village on the old Great North Road but now bypassed.

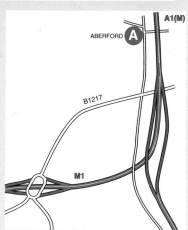

Places of interest
Lotherton Hall – 2m

The White Swan Hotel
Aberford
☎ 01132 813 205
Last orders: 2.30pm and 9.30,pm
10.30pm on Friday and Saturday nights.
££

It has been a coaching inn since 1720, when the Great North Road passed outside it. A rusting sign says that J. Heaton is licensed to rent post horses. It is a busy, noisy place full of mementoes and stuffed foxes. No dogs.

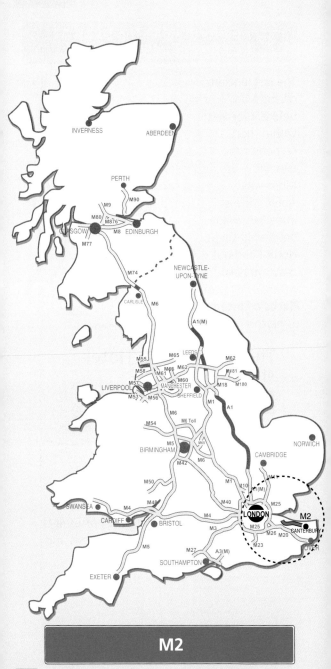

M2

London to Canterbury

Junctions   2 to 7

One of the shorter motorways, being 25 miles in length and was one of the first to be built in 1963. It was designed to make a fast link between London and the Channel Ports, although the approach to London remained abysmal. It has now been supplanted by the M20, with which you can interchange easily should the traffic become unbearable.

The motorway passes near some historic towns such as Rochester; the old Naval Dockyards at Chatham burnt by the Dutch and to the east the ancient city of Canterbury.

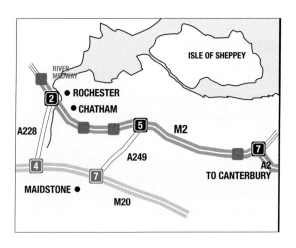

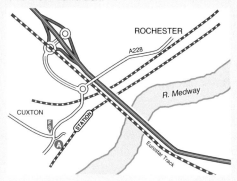

2 Rochester   West Malling
A228

At present it is the scene of construction work, building the Eurostar bridge over the Medway and the new railtrack.

ROCHESTER

A228

R. Medway

CUXTON

STATION

Eurostar Track

Places of interest
Rochester Castle (EH).
Gads Hill Place (HHA). Chatham Dockyard(EH).

 White Hart
Cuxton
☎ 01634 711 857
Last orders: 2.30pm and 9.30pm.
No evening meals on Sundays.
££

A managed pub of Shepherd Neame, it has a restaurant and bars serving bar meals. There is a playground and a beer garden where dogs can sit and children play.
A comfort stop.

| 5 | Sittingbourne & Sheerness A249
Maidstone A249 |

Easy enough to get to Stockbury, as there is a gap in the dual-carriageway, opposite the turning off.

Stockbury features in the Domesday Book as Stochinberge in 1086.

 The Harrow Inn
Stockbury
☎ 01795 842 546
Last orders: 2.00pm and 9.30pm.
£££

This typical country pub opposite the village green has been there since 1750. It is a Free House and serves bar meals and Hurlimann Swiss lager every day of the week. There is a beer garden at the rear where dogs and children can roam.

7 Dover   Channel Tunnel
Canterbury A2

The last junction on the motorway before it
becomes a dual carriageway to Dover. If you are
coming from London there is no difficulty in
getting to Boughton and rejoining the Dover road
on the other side of the village. Coming from
Dover, you can either drive up to the roundabout
and return, or else
bear off the A2
about 2 miles to
the south.
Boughton is an
attractive village
with old half-
timbered houses in
the vernacular
style of the Weald.

Ⓐ The Queens Head.

Boughton
☎ 01227 751 369
Last orders: 2.30pm and 9pm. No evening
meals on Sundays and Mondays.
££

There has been an inn on this site for the past
400 years and it is still a simple locals' pub. It
serves bar meals, which could be useful if you
are too early for the ferry. You can also pass
the time of day
playing Bat and Trap,
a Kentish game.
Dogs welcome.

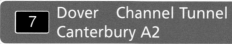

7 Dover   Channel Tunnel
Canterbury A2

B **The Garden Hotel and Restaurant**
Boughton
☎ 01227 751 411
Last orders: 2.00pm and 9.00pm.
No evening meals on Sundays.
££   🛏

An 18th Century house, which was a soup kitchen in the World War II, then an antique shop and for the past ten years a hotel with 10 bedrooms a restaurant and bar. It has just recently been refurbished. Soup is still on the menu, but there are a great many other choices.

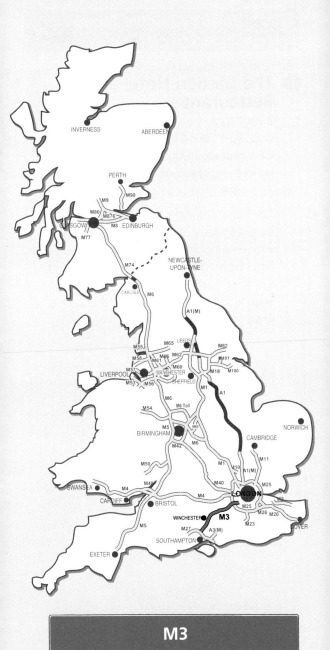

M3

London to Southampton

Junctions   3 to 14

This motorway connects London with the port of Southampton and with the south west of England by way of the A303.
The building of the continuation of the motorway past Winchester in 1994 meant the cutting of a trench through Twyford Down. This caused massive unrest (and cost) by protesters. It might have been cheaper in the long run to have tunnelled through.

We could find few places to eat in the southern section but Winchester is well worth a visit.

3 Guildford Bracknell A322 Lightwater

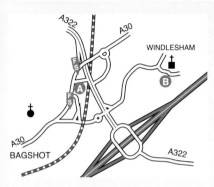

Bagshot has been expanded and therefore you could get lost in the streets. Just keep bearing to the right.

Ⓐ The Barn
Bagshot
☎ 01276 476 673
Last orders: Noon to 9.00pm.
£££

An open beamed barn with a collection of farming artifacts. It is now a restaurant which used to be and probably still is, much frequented by Officer Cadets from Sandhurst. It is family owned, where the food is cooked to order. There is some outside seating, where children are welcome but no dogs.

3 Guildford Bracknell A322
Lightwater

Half Moon
Windlesham
☎ 01276 473 329
Last orders: 3.00pm and 11.00pm.
On Sundays 10.30pm.
£££

A family run Free House which serves a
wide range of traditional food, beers and
fruit wines. As a result it has won the Beer
and Food Award. Home cooking in the
two bars which have a collection of RAF
prints. A large beer garden at the back
where dogs are welcome and a children's
playground. Facilities for the disabled,
regular park for horseboxes and caravans.

4a   Farnborough (W) A327 Fleet B3013

A simple junction and the pub is easy to find.

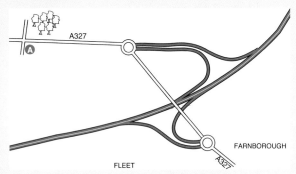

Places of interest

Napoleon III's Mausoleum, Farnborough – 3m
Airborne Forces Museum, Aldershot – 4m

Ⓐ Crown and Cushion
Yateley
☎ 01252 545 253
Last orders: 2.00pm and 8.30pm.
No evening meals on Sundays.
££

An attractive rural pub in a wooded area on the way to Yateley Common. It serves traditional meals in the bars and carvery, or else in the beer garden, which has heaters should the weather be inclement.
Dogs welcome.

5 Farnham A287

No real difficulty with this junction but take the road off the southern roundabout to North Warnborough.

Places of interest
Old Basing House – 5m

Blubeckers Eating House
North Warnborough
☎ 01256 702 953
Last orders: 2.30pm and 9.45pm
£££

This was once an old water mill and the mill pond makes an attractive setting for the restaurant, which has an imaginative menu. There is a playground, a family room and outside seating. Children welcome but no dogs.

Not a difficult junction and in fact you can get from one pub to the other under the Motorway should one of them be full.

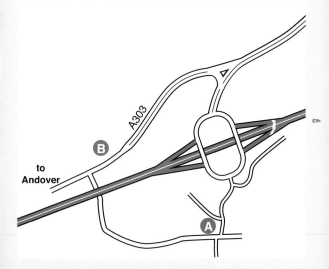

Places of interest
The Grange (EH) - 8m

7 Basingstoke A30
Newbury (A339)

A **Queen Inn** ✳
Dummer
☎ 01256 397 367
Last orders: 2.30pm and 9.30pm.
9.00pm on Sundays.
£££

A popular and well known family owned
pub. It gets its name from the fourth wife
of Henry VIII who was Anne of Cleves,
the Mare of
Flanders. There
is a garden
at the back
where dogs
are welcome.

B **Sun Inn**
Nr Dummer
☎ 01256 397 234
Last orders: 2.30pm and 9.00pm
9.30pm on Fridays and Saturdays.
££

Once a Coaching inn on the old Andover
road, it is now owned by a Group and
modernised. It has outside seating and a
beer garden where
dogs and children
are welcome.
A comfort
stop.

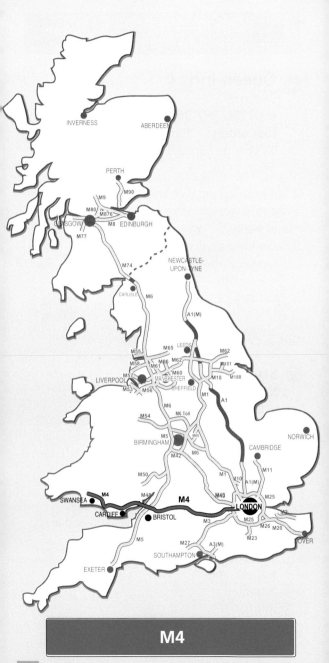

M4

London to South Wales

Junctions   4 to 48

The M4, which is 121 miles long, is the fourth longest motorway in the UK. It is a direct link from London to South Wales and interconnects with the M5 north of Bristol. The first section, the Chiswick Flyover, was opened in 1959 by a blonde starlet. The last part to be completed was in 1973. It may be continued to Fishguard at some future date, instead of terminating in a rather bleak part of South Wales. It passes through some of the most varied scenery in Southern England.

EASTERN SECTION   8/9 to 14

This section of the motorway follows along the Thames valley past Reading and Newbury before rising up to the open expanses of the Marlborough Downs.

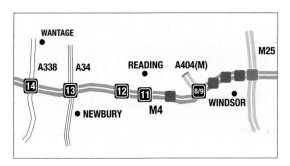

8/9 Maidenhead Windsor A308
Bracknell A308
Henley High Wycombe A4(M)

Coming off at the junction take the motorway spur to the roundabout. Then follow the signs to Holyport and turn left at the village green. The Belgian Arms is on the left at the end of the green.
For the Shire Horse, take the A404 (M) and turn left at the roundabout.

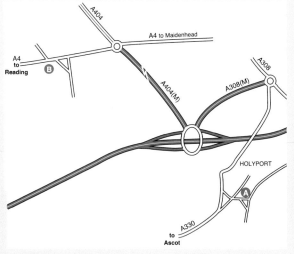

Places of interest
Dorney Court (HHA) – 2m
Windsor Castle (Her Majesty The Queen) – 5m

8/9 Maidenhead Windsor A308
Bracknell A308
Henley High Wycombe A4(M)

Ⓐ The Belgian Arms
Holyport
☎ 01628 634 468
Last orders: 2.00pm and 9.30pm.
No evening meals on Sundays.
£££

A popular pub on the edge of the village green by a duck pond which ducks still use. There is a large garden by the pond where you can sit in the summer and dogs can play.

Ⓑ The Shire Horse
Littlewick Green
☎ 01628 825 335
Last orders: 10.00pm.
9.00pm on Sundays.
££

The pub, part of Scottish and Newcastle, has open beamed and brick areas serving bar meals. Outside there is a beer garden and children's playground. No dogs. Facilities for the disabled.

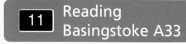

11 Reading
Basingstoke A33

At the roundabout turn left to Three Mile Cross,
but avoid getting onto the dual carriageway.

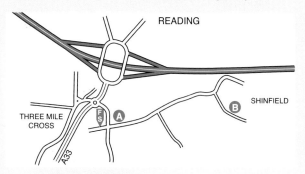

Places of interest
Stratfield Saye (HHA) – 5m
Silchester (Calleva Atrebartum) – 7m

Ⓐ The Swan

Three Mile Cross
☎ 01189 883 674
Last orders: 10.00pm. Closed Sunday
evenings. *££*

Traditional Free House with a restaurant for
lunches on weekdays, as well as serving bar
meals washed down with Real Ales. There is
some outside seating and a beer garden
beyond the large car park. The resident Irish
Wolfhound, Jumbo, is the mascot of the
London Irish Rugby Football Club.

11 Reading
Basingstoke A33

Ⓑ **L'Ortolan Restaurant** *
Shinfield
☎ 01189 883 783
Last orders: 2.30pm and 10.00pm.
No evening meals on Sundays.
££££

It was once an old vicarage with a large
garden but has now been converted into
a comfortable, Michelin starred
restaurant, specialising in classical French
cuisine. It is efficient with attentive service
in comfortable surroundings. A
conservatory where you can have a drink
before lunch or coffee afterwards.

12 Theale
Reading A4

At the roundabout turn right to Theale, which is a surprisingly attractive little town. It is so named as it was the second night's stop out of London for wagoners and was called The Ale. It certainly seems to have more than its fair share of pubs and hotels, so if the one mentioned below is full, there are probably alternatives.

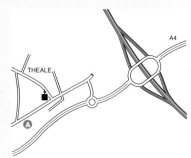

Places of interest
Engelfield House Garden (HHA) – 3m
Basildon Park (NT) – 4m

Ⓐ The Volunteer
Theale
☎ 01189 302 489
Last orders: Noon to 9.00pm
2.30pm on Sundays.
££

Traditional old pub, serving bar meals with home cooking. There is outside seating and a car park at the rear. An interesting collection of military and sporting prints.
No dogs indoors.

M4

13 Newbury A34 Oxford

Ye Olde Red Lion is easy to find. For the Red House follow the plan as indicated and keep going.

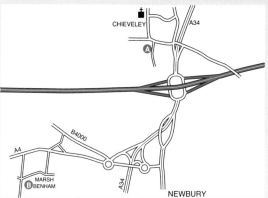

 Ye Olde Red Lion
Chieveley
☎ 01635 248 379
Last orders: 2.30pm and 9.30pm.
ff

An award winning village pub.
It has a restaurant with an imaginative menu and a bar with a collection of curios. Log fires inside and benches outside for those wanting fresh air. Children and dogs are welcome but there is a resident dog.

13 Newbury A34   Oxford

B **The Red House** *

Marsh Benham
☎ 01635 582 017
Last orders: 2.15pm and 9.30pm.
No evening meals on Sunday.
Closed Mondays.
££££

A privately owned elegant restaurant in a
thatched house, with an adjoining bar.
Outside seating in a garden with its own
carpark. English and Continental cuisine
using local produce either a la carte in the
Restaurant or with a Bistro menu. Children
and dogs welcome but preferably outside.
Well worth the additional minutes to get
there.

14 Hungerford   Wantage A338

An easy junction. Follow the sign to Lambourn
for the Pheasant Inn.

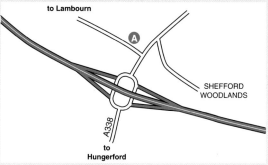

Places of interest
Ashdown House (NT) – 11m

 ## The Pheasant Inn *
Shefford Woodlands
☎ 01488 648 284
Last orders: 2.30pm and 9.00pm.
9.30pm on Fridays and Saturdays.
Open Sunday evenings.
£££

An historic wooden framed building. It has
always been a popular rendezvous and has
recently been renovated. It includes a
restaurant with an excellent chef, so food
is taken seriously and good bar snacks are
available. It is a pleasant place, especially
for the racing fraternity.
Outside seating
in a garden.

MIDDLE SECTION **15** to **23**

This part of the motorway descends from the open chalk Downs towards Junction 15 and Swindon. From there it is rolling countryside as far as the Severn Bridge.

Swindon was the centre of the locomotive workshops for the Great Western Railway but is now a modern commercial town with a railway museum. Chippenham was once a picturesque market town but has now been modernised out of all recognition. Bath, off Junction 18, is famous for its Georgian architecture. The old docks and SS Great Britain in Bristol are also worth a visit.

In 1996 the second Severn Bridge was completed to cope with the increased traffic. The older bridge crossing was then renamed the M48 and the new section became the M4. The M49 link to Avonmouth is best avoided if seeking a meal.

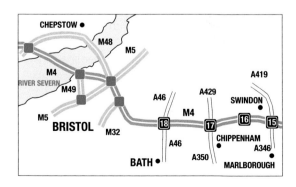

15   Swindon A419   Oxford (A420) Marlborough A364

There is a clutch of pubs in this area, who probably did a roaring trade when Chiseldon was an airforce base, and then an American military hospital.

Places of interest

Ashdown House (NT) – 7m; Waylands Smithy – 8m; Barbury Castle – 5m

Plough Inn

Badbury

☎ 01793 740 342

Last orders: 2.00pm and 9.00pm.

££

A busy roadside pub dating from 1864 owned by Arkells Brewery. It has a restaurant and a bar, childrens playground, beer garden and its own car park. Coffee is available for the passing motorist. Dogs are welcome.

15   Swindon A419 Oxford (A420)
Marlborough A364

B Chiseldon House Hotel
Chiseldon
☎ 01793 741 010
Last orders: 2.00pm and 9.15pm.
£££   🛏

A fine 19th Century manor house, which has
been converted into a privately owned hotel.
It has 21 bedrooms, extensive gardens and a
peaceful setting.
Children and dogs are welcome.
It has the Orangery
Restaurant and a bar.
Bar meals and morning
coffee for the casual
visitor.

C Patriots Arms
Chiseldon
☎ 01793 740 331
Last orders: 2.00pm and 9.00pm
££   🛏

It has been a pub since 1840 and is now a Free
House with 2 bedrooms, a restaurant and bar.
Outside there is a beer garden and a children's
playground. Inside there is a family room for
wet days. A large
carpark at rear.
Dogs however
are not
welcome.

16 Swindon   Wootton Bassett Calne A3102

An uninspiring junction but easy enough to find the pub, which is before you get into Wootton Bassett.

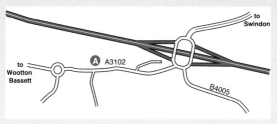

Places of interest
Lydiard Park (Swindon B.C.) – 1m

 ## Sally Pussey's Inn
Nr Wootton Bassett
☎ 01793 852 430
Last orders: 8.00am to 9.30pm.
££

Do not be too put off by the formidable woman portrayed on the inn sign, as the welcome inside is friendly. It has been fully modernised to have a Steak and Carvery Restaurant as well as a bar, which also serves meals.

17 Chippenham A350
Cirencester A429

Most of the pubs are easy to find, but the Hit and Miss in Kington Langley could be missed which would be a pity. Take the narrow road when you come off the roundabout.

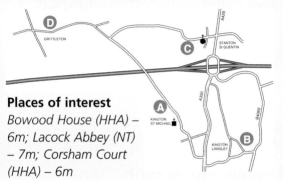

Places of interest
*Bowood House (HHA) –
6m; Lacock Abbey (NT)
– 7m; Corsham Court
(HHA) – 6m*

The Jolly Huntsman
Kington St Michael
☎ 01249 750 305
Last orders: 2.00.pm and 9.30pm
9.00pm on Sundays.
ff 🛏

A popular locals' pub in this attractive village. Well known for its Real Ales of which there are at least 6 different varieties.
There are 6 double bedrooms for those who might wish to drink to the full.
Log fires and home made bar meals. Some outside seating and dogs are welcomed by the amiable owners.
It stays open for
365 days of
the year.

17 Chippenham A350
Cirencester A429

Ⓑ The Hit and Miss *
Kington Langley
☎ 01249 758 830
Last orders: 2.30pm and 9.30pm.
8.30pm on Sundays.
££

A popular village pub dating from the 18th
Century in the centre of this scattered
hamlet. There is a friendly welcome to all
including dogs and it has an imaginative
menu. A good ambiance.
Some outside
seating for summer
use. It specialises
in sea food.

Ⓒ Stanton Manor Hotel
Stanton St Quintin
☎ 01666 837 552
Last orders: 2.00pm and 9.30pm
££

A privately owned hotel, set in 7 acres of
garden. It has 23 bedrooms, most in a
modern annexe. Children welcome but dogs
by arrangement. Bar meals are served but
there is the Gallery Restaurant with an
imaginative menu and an eclectic mix of
paintings for sale.

Neeld Arms
Grittleton
☎ 01249 782 470
Last orders: 2.00.pm and 9.30pm
£££ 🛏

A Free House which has recently been taken
over by Charlie West.
It was a locals' village pub but is being
improved with two Portuguese chefs providing
traditional meals with hints of the Iberian
peninsula.
6 comfortably furnished bedrooms, one of
them in the attic space under a tangle of roof
trusses.
A cheerful and friendly place and ideal for
those coming to Mary Howard's Gift Fair in
Hullavington.

18 Bath   Stroud A46

An easy junction and not difficult to find the various places.

Places of interest
Dyrham Park(NT) – 1m
Horton Court (HHA) – 5m

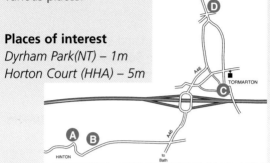

A Hinton Grange Hotel
Hinton
☎ 01179 372 916
Last orders: 2.00.pm and 9.15pm
££££   🛏   🍷

Once a farmhouse built in 1614 and enlarged in 1750, it is surrounded by a lake and garden.
It could be described as a quirky experience in comfort, to include open fires in the bedrooms of which there are 19.
It has a restaurant and a bar in the conservatory.
Dogs are welcome.

18　Bath　Stroud A46

B Bull Inn
Hinton
☎ 01179 372 332
Last orders: 2.00.pm and 9.00pm
No evening meals on Sundays and closed
Monday lunch.
£££

A friendly village pub with two large fireplaces
for winter nights.
There is a no smoking
restaurant, outside
seating, a large garden
and playground.
All food cooked on
the premises. Children
and dogs welcome.
Parking for horseboxes.

C The Portcullis Inn
Tormarton
☎ 01454 218 263
Last orders: 2.30pm and 9.45pm
££　🛏

A friendly, old fashioned, privately owned
village pub, with 6 bedrooms. There is a dining
area and a bar which serves an excellent steak
and kidney pie, so much so that it is now an
essential stopping off point for Czech tourists.
The resident
dog is not too
keen on
canine visitors.

18 Bath Stroud A46

D Cross Hands Hotel
Old Sodbury
☎ 01454 313 000
Last orders: 2.30pm and 10.30pm.
10.00pm on Sundays.
£££ 🛏

An old Coaching Inn which used to be a
livery stable for those coming down for a
day out with the Beaufort Hunt. It is an
ingenious mix of new and old and some
of the 15 bedrooms still reflect those
bygone days, as not all of them have
bathrooms attached.
There is a restaurant and the bars also
serve bar meals and morning coffee.
A claim to fame is that the Queen had to
spend the night there in 1981 when
marooned in a snow storm. Dogs are
welcome, especially corgis.

WELSH SECTION   **23a** to **48**

As the map suggests there are few places where it is worth leaving the motorway to eat. There are however plenty of places to see off the motorway.

Caerleon off Junction 24 is the site of Isca, the Roman base of the II (Augusta) Legion from Spain.

In Cardiff, the regional capital of Wales, the Castle is built on the walls of the Roman fort whilst to the north there is Castell Coch, both restored by the 3rd Marquis of Bute in the nineteenth century with the help of the architect William Burges.

Some six miles beyond Castell Coch to the east are the imposing ruins of Caerphilly Castle, mute evidence of the occupation by Edward I.

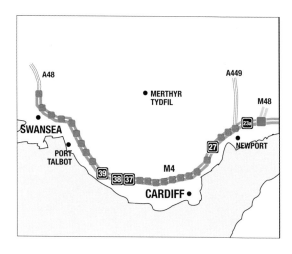

23a Magor B4245 Caldicott

A slightly complicated junction. The approach to the village can confuse the direction to the pub.

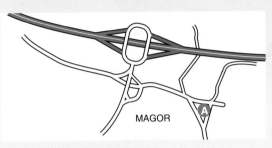

Places of interest
Penhow Castle (HHA) – 2m

Ⓐ Wheatsheaf

Magor
☎ 01633 880 608
Last orders: Noon to 9.30pm.
3.00pm on Sundays.
£ 🛏

Some two hundred years old, it has a large modernised open plan restaurant and bars downstairs where home made food is served. Upstairs there are 5 bedrooms. Some outside seating. Dogs are not permitted.

27   High Cross   B4591

Take the B4591 road north to Risca and Abertillery.
After about a mile the Rising Sun is on the left.

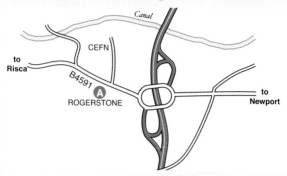

Ⓐ The Rising Sun
Rogerstone
☎ 01633 895 126
Last orders: 2.15pm and 9.30pm.
No evening meals on Sundays.
££   🛏

A family run pub with a good reputation. It has
a two storey conservatory at the rear of the
restaurant, with two large bars elsewhere.
The menu is imaginative with self service at
lunch. Children welcome but not dogs. A
surprise to find a deservedly popular place
which looks unassuming at first sight.

| 37 | North Cornelly A48 Porthcawl A4228 |

This could be complicated if you do not follow the plan. Follow the signs to Kenfig. If the Angel is full the Prince of Wales in the village is an unaltered locals' pub.

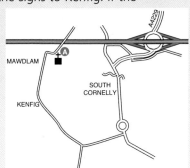

 The Angel
Mawdlam
☎ 01656 740 456
Last orders: 2.30pm and 9.00pm
No evening meals on Sundays.
£ 🍺

A tenanted pub of Enterprises Inns. It has been refurbished, but is a friendly place with views along the coast. It specialises in fish and house baked fare. There are three bedrooms. Plenty of outside seating where dogs are encouraged as well as children. Car park to cope with horseboxes.

38/39 Port Talbot A48

Going east there is no problem about exiting
and entering again, but driving west, you have
to take the dual carriageway for a short
distance before joining the motorway again.

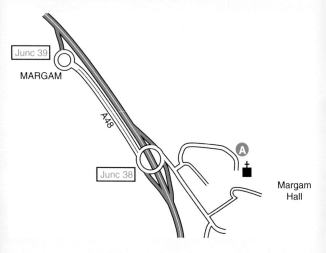

Places of interest
Margam Park (HHA) – 1m
The Stones Museum – ½m
Margam Abbey – ½m

38/39 Port Talbot A48

(A) **The Abbots Kitchen and Restaurant**
Margam
☎ 01639 871 184
Last orders: 4.00pm. 2.30pm on Sundays.
£

A haven of peace shielded from the steel works in Port Talbot by woodland. The whole area was part of an Early Norman abbey. The church was 'restored' by the Victorians, but nevertheless it is still a fine building, where services are held. Next door is the Stones Museum with a good collection of inscribed Celtic stones.

The Abbots Kitchen is in the stables of Margam House where tea, coffee and cakes or a light lunch are provided until 4pm. Dogs and children welcome.

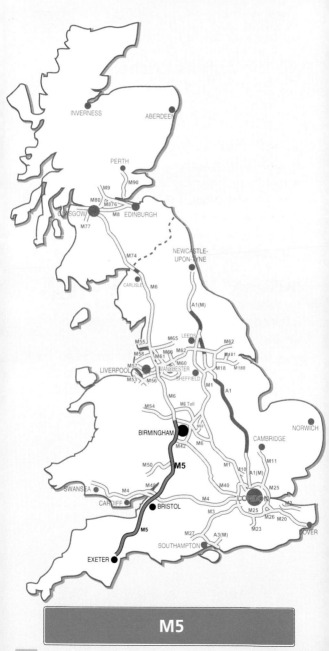

M5

Birmingham to Exeter

Junctions 3 to 31

The M5 is 168 miles in length and was built in sections, the first part being completed in 1969 and the last in 1976. It was designed to link the Midlands with the South West, via Bristol.

It is one of the few Motorways which has no connection with London. Considering that it passes through some of the prettiest of the English countryside, it is poorly served for looking after the needs of motorists.

NORTHERN SECTION 1 to 10

A boring stretch of motorway until you get south of Worcester.

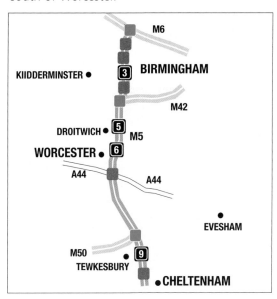

3 Kidderminster A456
Birmingham (W and Cen) A456

A straightforward junction. Just follow the dual carriageway until you see the pub. You will have to get back to the junction by going round the roundabout.

Places of interest
Hagley Hall (HHA) – 5m; Halesowen Abbey – 1m

 The Black Horse
Halesowen
☎ 0121 550 1465
Last orders: 2.00pm and 10.00pm.
9.30pm on Sundays.
££

An outlet of the Spirit Group and now modernised to serve bar meals. Outside seating, where dogs are allowed.

5 Droitwich   Bromsgrove A38

The roundabouts tend to confuse but look out
for the signs to Droitwich

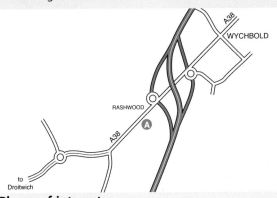

Places of interest
Hanbury Hall (NT) – 3m

 ## Robin Hood
Rashwood
☎ 01527 861 931
Last orders: 9.30pm. 10pm on Saturdays.
9pm on Sundays.
££

A Bass owned pub, it is deservedly well
known to the passing motorist. Outside
seating and a beer garden at the rear,
where dogs are allowed.

6   Worcester   Evesham A4538
Kidderminster A449

Follow the plan so
as not to
overshoot the
turning to the
right.

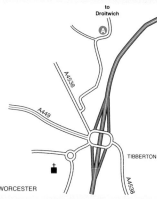

Places of interest   WORCESTER
Worcester Cathedral – 3m
*Dyson Perrins Museum (Royal Worcester porcelain)
– 2m*

Ⓐ The Pear Tree
Smite
☎ 01905 756 565
Last orders: 2.30pm and 9.30pm.
£££

A 24 bedroomed hotel and conference centre,
which was converted and enlarged some ten
years ago. The original house dating from the
18th century is where you can now have bar
meals. Fresh fish a speciality. No dogs.

9   Tewkesbury A438
Evesham A46

A simple junction. Just keep going until you see the tower of the Abbey. It is a picturesque old market town with some fine buildings.

Places of interest
Tewkesbury Abbey

Ye Olde Black Bear
Tewkesbury
☎ 01684 292 202
Last orders: 9.00pm.
No evening meals on Sunday.
££

Said to be the oldest pub in Gloucestershire, dating from 1308. It has a beer garden at the rear on the banks of the Lower Avon Navigation Canal where dogs are allowed. Bar meals are served throughout the day.

> **9** Tewkesbury A438
> Evesham A46

Ⓐ The Royal Hop Pole
Tewkesbury
☎ 01684 293 236
Last orders: 2.00pm and 9.00pm.
9.30pm on Fridays and Saturdays.
No evening meals on Sundays.
£££ 🛏

It is a comfortable old fashioned hotel. No one seems to know the origin of the name but it dates from the 15th century. It is also famous as the place where Dickens wrote that Pickwick spent the night there! There are 29 bedrooms, most facing on to a well tended garden leading down to the river Avon. A restaurant and a friendly bar.

Birmingham to Exeter

M5

MIDDLE SECTION   **11a** to **21**

This stretch takes you from Cheltenham and Gloucester, with its historic cathedral where Edward II is buried, to south of Bristol. The motorway passes through pleasant countryside and there are interesting houses and places to see along the River Severn. South of the crossing with the M4, Junction 18 is the best turn off for Bristol and Kings Weston House, designed by Sir John Vanbrugh. You can drive along the Avon Gorge, under Brunel's Clifton Suspension Bridge and then into Bristol with its restored dockside and the SS Great Britain.

During the summer the stretch from the M4 intersection south to the bridge over the Avon can get gridlocked.

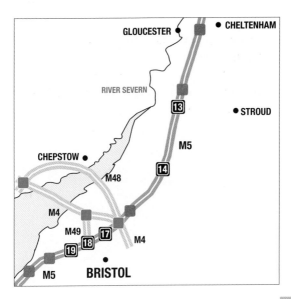

13   Stroud A419
Dursley

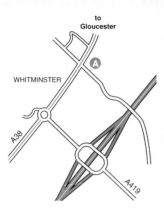

An easy junction.

Places of interest

*Hardwicke Court
(HHA) – 3m
Wildfowl and
Wetlands Centre
(Slimbridge) – 6m
Frampton Manor – 3m*

Ⓐ **The Old Forge** ✳

Whitminster

☎ 01452 741 306

Last orders: 2.00pm and 9.00pm.

No evening meals on Sundays and Mondays

££

The building is dated 1604 and must have been a smithy if the name is to be believed. It is a Free House and has a cheerful and friendly atmosphere with a small low beamed but airy restaurant. There is outside seating and dogs are welcome.

14   Thornbury
Dursley B4509

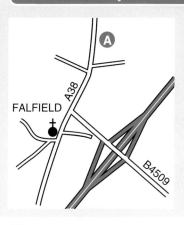

An uncomplicated junction.

Places of interest
Berkeley Castle (HHA) – 5m

Ⓐ The Gables
Falfield
☎ 01454 260 502
Last orders: 2.00pm for bar meals only.
9.30pm in the bar and restaurant.
£££

The Gables was once a wayside pub. It has now been rebuilt as an hotel with 46 bedrooms, a restaurant, bar and a fitness gym for those wanting a workout or relaxing from a conference. It has recently changed hands.

17   Bristol A4018
       Cribbs Causeway

Easy enough to find the way, especially if in need of a comfort stop. Good view towards the Severn Bridges.

 The Fox

Easter Compton
☎ 01454 632 220
Last orders: 2.00pm and 9.30pm.
No evening meals on Sundays.
££

A simple village pub with a garden and children's playground. Morning coffee can be had if in a rush. Under 14s not allowed in the bars.

18 Bristol A4
Avonmouth and Docks (A403)

The exit is complicated as it gets snarled up with the junction of the M49. Follow the A4 Portway sign. At Shirehampton turn left up Kings Weston Avenue. After passing the remains of a Roman Villa on the right, turn right up the hill marked Kings Weston Lane. The entrance gates are at the top of the hill on the right. Alternatively drive on until you can see the brown signs for Kings Weston.

Places of interest
SS Great Britain – 4m; Bristol Docks – 4m

Ⓐ Kings Weston House *

Kings Weston
☎ 01179 382 299
Last orders: 10am to 4pm every day.
£

It is not every motorist who can have a light lunch or a traditional tea in a house designed by Sir John Vanbrugh.

It has now been renovated to cater for conferences and functions. The Tea Room below, with its own entrance complete with a Vanbrugh fireplace, is open to passing motorists. There is a large park for walking the dog.

19 Clifton Portishead A369
Royal Portbury Dock (Toll)

The Rudgleigh Inn is easy to find.

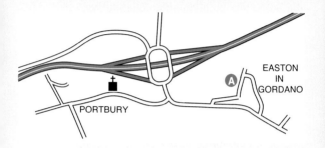

The Kings Arms

Easton in Giordano
☎ 01275 372 208
Last orders: 2.00pm and 9.00pm. 8.00pm on
Sundays.
£

A simple tenanted village pub with flagstoned
floors and carpeted areas serving bar meals
and sandwiches. A friendly place for villagers
and motorists. Outside seating and a beer
garden. Car park. Dogs and children allowed.

Birmingham to Exeter

SOUTHERN SECTION 22 to 31

South of Bristol the motorway winds between the Mendip Hills before crossing the flat levels of Sedgemoor, remembered for the defeat of the Duke of Monmouth and the Bloody Assizes of Judge Jeffreys.

Glastonbury, famous for the supposed site of the Holy Grail and also for the annual pop concert, is close to the motorway.

Taunton is an attractive county town, with a good antique market. The motorway ends south of Exeter, which was once a Roman city, with a fine medieval cathedral. It continues as dual- carriageway to Plymouth and Cornwall.

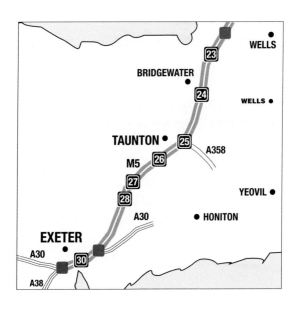

23 Glastonbury   Wells (A39)
Highbridge A38

The Puriton Inn is signed just off the junction
on the left.

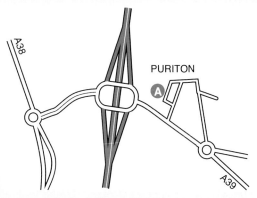

Places of interest
Glastonbury Abbey – 13m

Ⓐ The Puriton Inn
Puriton
☎ 01278 683 464
Last orders: 2.30pm and 9.30pm.
9.00pm on Sundays.
£

A 200 year old village pub with a Skittle Alley.
It takes pride in its home cooking. There is a
children's playground and outside seating,
where dogs are permitted.
Car park.

24 Bridgwater A38
Minehead (A39)

The junction is easy enough, but the road to Huntworth is twisty and narrow - keep on over a narrow wooden bridge.

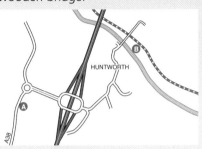

Places of interest

Maunsel Grange Garden (HHA) – 2m

Ⓐ The Boat and Anchor Inn

Huntworth

☎ 01278 662 473

Last orders: May-Oct.From noon-9.00pm
Oct-May. 3,00 & 9.00pm

££

The reason for the name soon becomes apparent as the beer garden is on the banks of the Bridgwater and Taunton Canal. It has 3 bedrooms which are double glazed, a restaurant and a long bar. Coffee is served to thirsty bargees as well as something stronger. Children and dogs are welcome, if kept on a lead.

24　Bridgewater A38
Minehead

Ⓑ The Compass Tavern
North Petherton
☎ 01278 662 283
Last orders: 3.00pm and 9.00pm on
Saturdays and Sundays. 12.00pm to 9.00pm.
££

A 16th century pub, which specialises in home
cooking in a large open beamed dining area
but pay heed to the notices to mind your step
or mind your head. Friendly atmosphere with
home cooked food and real ales. Outside
seating and a large beer garden where dogs
are welcome. The car park will take
horseboxes.

25 Taunton Honiton Yeovil Weymouth A358

An easy junction being the main turn off for Taunton. The Hankridge Arms is in the middle of a retail shopping area so head for Sainsburys!

RUISHTON

Places of interest
Hestercombe House Gardens (HHA) – 3m

Ⓐ Blackbrook Tavern
Ruishton
☎ 01823 443 121
Last orders: 10.00pm. 9.30pm on Sundays.
££

Owned by a Group it is a busy pub of beams and bricks, on the outskirts of Taunton, with 38 double bedrooms, a restaurant in a large conservatory and bars. There is a children's playground as well as outside seating.
Dogs are not welcome.

25 Taunton Honiton Yeovil
Weymouth A358

B The Hankridge Arms
Taunton
☎ 01823 444 405
Last orders: All day to 9.30pm.
£££

Once an Elizabethan farmhouse of some
importance, it was rescued from dereliction by
the Hall and Woodhouse Brewery at some
considerable cost. No soon was it completed
than it was surrounded by a shopping precinct.
It is however a comfortable and friendly place
with all the original features still retained to
include a bar and a restaurant. Large car park.

Birmingham to Exeter

26 Wellington A38
Taunton

Turn right on the roundabout on the A38.
Wellington is a pleasant country town but
nothing special in the way of places to eat. The
return to the motorway from the Blackbird via
West Buckland is not recommended, as the
roads are narrow and you could get lost.

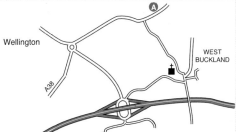

Places of interest
Cothay Manor Gardens (HHA) – 6m

Ⓐ The Blackbird ∗
West Buckland
☎ 018223 461 273
Last orders: 2.00pm and 9.30pm.
No evening meals on Sundays.
££ 🛏

A Free House, it prides itself on the home
cooking, served in the bar and in the
restaurant which has lace table cloths. It
also has 2 bedrooms for the overnight
motorist. Outside there outside seating
but dog owners are warned that there are
two large
resident
dogs.
Children
welcome.

27 Tiverton Barnstaple A361
Wellington A38

Getting there is easy enough but the return is more
difficult with what seems to be a needlessly
complicated system of roundabouts.

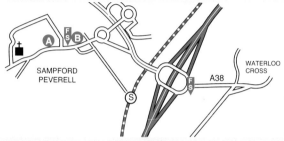

Places of interest
Knightshayes Court.(NT) – 6m

Ⓐ The Globe Inn
Sampford Peverell
☎ 01884 821 214
Last orders: 2.00pm and 10.00pm.
££

A popular pub with a restaurant and bars as
well as 6 double bedrooms. There is a
children's playground and a beer garden at the
rear. Dogs are welcome, and there are facilities
for the disabled. A skittle alley for
use on wet days.

A ## The Parkway House Country Hotel
Sampford Peverell
☎ 01884 820 255
Last orders: 2.00pm and 9.30pm
Dinner on Sundays for Residents only.
£££ 🛏 🍷

Built between the wars as a family house,
it became a doctors surgery until the
1960s. It is now a family owned and run
hotel with attentive and friendly service. It
has 10 bedrooms, an airy conservatory
and a restaurant.
Children welcome and dogs by
arrangement.
Car parking for caravans and horseboxes.

28 Honiton A373
Cullompton B3181

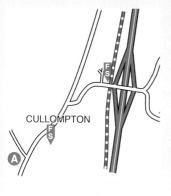

Slightly complicated by having a Motorway Service Station just off the junction. There is also another filling station on the way into Cullompton, which is an attractive town. You may miss the road back to the motorway by continuing north.

Ⓐ Manor House Hotel
Cullompton
☎ 01884 322 281
Last orders: 2.30pm and 9.30pm.
Lunch only on Sundays.
££ 🛏

A 17th Century town house which must once have been of some importance. It has changed hands with part having 9 bedrooms and a restaurant and on the other side there is a public bar which has not been renovated. Outside seating and a car park at the rear.

30 Exeter Dawlish A376
Exmouth A376 Sidmouth A3052

The village is not difficult to find. To get to the Blue Ball Inn, you will have to go up to the roundabout and return as there is no break in the dual carriageway.

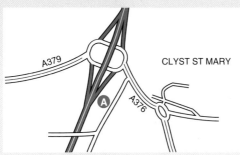

A379

CLYST ST MARY

A376

Ⓐ **A** **Blue Ball Inn** ✶
Sandygate
☎ 01392 873 401
Last orders: 2.30pm and 9.30pm
9.00pm on Sundays.
£££

An attractive 18th Century pub in a quiet lane, with scrubbed tables, tiled floors, low beamed ceilings and home cooking. Coffee and teas can also be had. There is a large garden, but dogs are not welcome. It is about to be enlarged.

M6 and M6 (Toll)

M6 (toll)

This is the latest addition to the motorway network and was opened in 2004.
Built by private enterprise under the aegis of the last government, it should certainly be an improvement to the endless traffic jams at Spaghetti Junction which could add hours to journey times.
At first glance the route does not seem to bode well for finding places just off the junctions, but there are some amongst the area north of Birmingham.
For golfing enthusiasts there is the De Vere Belfry Hotel just off junction 2, but access there is restricted. Another snag is that to regain access to the motorway you will have to pay another toll charge.

T4 Burton   Lichfield A38
Tamworth A5   North M42

Take the A38 to
Lichfield. After about
half a mile there is a gap
in the central reservation
and a sign for Swinfen.
Pass two signs – one
saying Swinfen Hall
Hotel, the other saying
Her Majesty's Young
Offenders Institute
Swinfen or HM. YOI for
short.

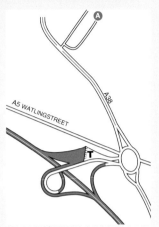

Ⓐ Swinfen Hall Hotel *
Swinfen
☎ 01543 481 494
Last orders: 2.30pm and 9.30pm.
££££

The original part of the house was built in
1757 to the design of Benjamin Wyatt. The
Swinfens lived there until 1948, when it passed
to the Government.
Once derelict it has now been converted into
an elegant hotel with 19 bedrooms and bars.
The Ballroom was built in 1910 for the
wedding of the only daughter who eloped
three weeks beforehand.
Children welcome
but dogs in
cars overnight.

T5 Lichefield A5148 Burton (A38)

There is no access to Shenstone and only an exit if drivng west. Best to get off at Junction 4.

Ⓐ The Bulls Head
Shenstone
☎ 01543 480 214
Last orders: 10pm every day. 9.30 on Sundays.
££

A managed house of Mitchells and Butlers. It has had a company makeover but still retains a friendly, folksy atmosphere with restaurant areas and bars.
Outside seating and a large car park at rear.
Children welcome but dogs outside.

Junctions   1 to 44

A first trial section of a motorway was built as the Preston Bypass in 1958, before the M1 was finished in 1959. The M6 is one of the longest motorways, being some 180 miles in length. It was built over a period of years, starting in 1962 and the last section was finished in 1972. The link over the Scottish Border connecting up with the M74 is still to be completed.

SOUTHERN SECTION   1 to 14

This section of the motorway is dull and when combined with the inevitable snarl up at Spaghetti Junction it becomes downright tedious. It gets better just south of Stafford. The opening of the new M6 (Toll) should improve matters.

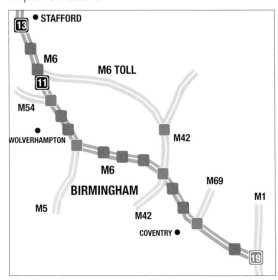

11　Wolverhampton Cannock A460

On the way to Shareshill there is a filling station but it only sells diesel.
For those driving from the north and wanting to go to Shrewsbury, turn off here to get to the M54.
The new M6 (Toll) joins the M6 at Junction 11A half a mile to the north

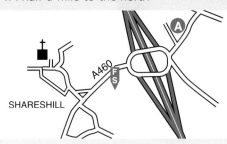

 The Wheatsheaf
Laney Green
☎ 01922 412 304
Last orders: from 12.00pm to 9.00pm.
8.00pm on Sundays.
£

Once an old roadside pub, it has now been modernised, with a conservatory style dining area. Bar meals served. Children's playground, a garden and plenty of parking for caravans and horseboxes.

M6 (toll)

Head for Action Trussell and keep going through the village. The Moat House is to the right on the village green.

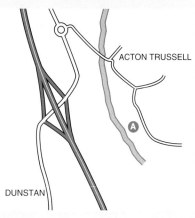

ACTON TRUSSELL

Ⓐ

DUNSTAN

Places of interest
Shugborough Hall (NT) – 8m

Ⓐ The Moat House Hotel

Acton trussell
☎ 01785 712 217
Last orders: 2.15pm and 9.30pm.
£££ 🛏

The hotel is still surrouned by part of the moat and the fireplace of the original 15th century structure is in the present bar, next to the restaurant. It has now been enlarged into a modern hotel along the banks of the canal but bar meals are available. A conference centre as well so a large car park suitable for horse boxes. Children allowed but no dogs.

MIDDLE SECTION 15 to 32

Stoke on Trent is the home of pottery, which is attractive but the same could not be said for the town itself. Nearby Barlaston Hall was built in 1756 by Sir Robert Taylor for the Wedgwoods as their home and factory. It was shamefully neglected by the firm until saved at the last moment by SAVE Britain's Heritage.

The countryside in Cheshire is pleasant enough but once over the Manchester Ship Canal, the surroundings are more crowded with motorways. It is small wonder that the local inhabitants were beginning to complain as more and more of their land was being taken to build yet another motorway.

17 Congleton Sandbach A534

Look out for Church Lane, which is made obvious by the Church.

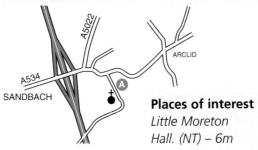

Places of interest
Little Moreton Hall. (NT) – 6m

Ⓐ The Chimney House Hotel
Sandbach
☎ 01270 764 141
Last orders: 2.00pm and 10.00pm,
9.30pm on Sundays.
£££

It was once the Rectory, but is now converted to a modern hotel with 48 bedrooms and a conference centre with appropriate car parking. A comfortable restaurant but the lounge bar also serves snacks. There is outside seating and eight acres of woodland. Children but no dogs allowed. Breakfast can be available.

18 Northwich Middlewich Chester Holmes Chapel A54

No difficulty with this junction.

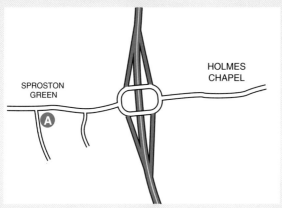

Places of interest
Capesthorne Hall. (HHA) – 9m

The Fox and Hounds

Sproston Green
☎ 01606 832 303
Last orders: 2.30pm and 9.00pm.
8.00pm on Sundays. Closed Monday
nights.
££

A wayside pub now owned by the Pub
Mistress Group. It has a restaurant and
bars with flagged floors, beamed ceilings
and a bowling green now out of use. A
beer garden where children and dogs are
welcome.

19 Manchester   Macclesfield A556
Northwich   Knutsford A537

The road to Fryers Nurseries can be on the minor roads or further on and turn right on the main road. The Smoker at Plumley may seem to be a bit far.

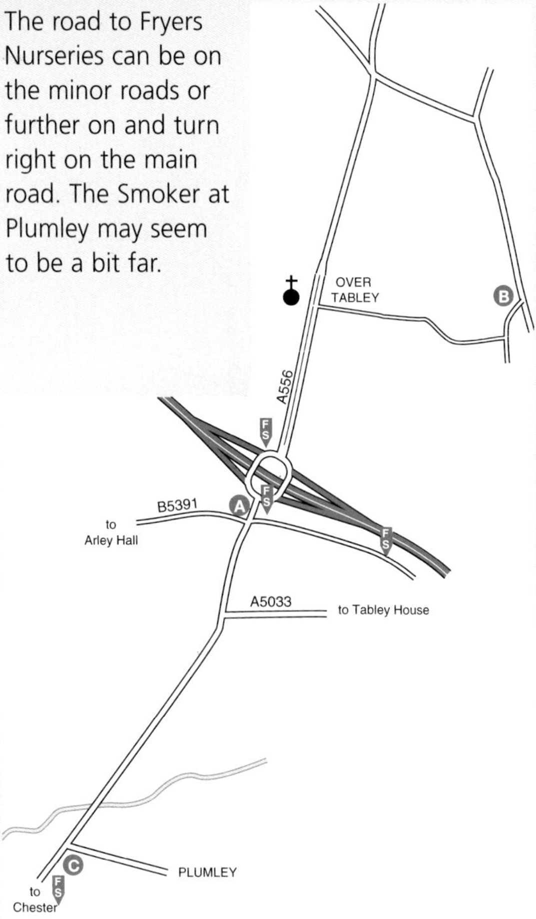

OVER TABLEY

B

A556

B5391

to Arley Hall

A

A5033 — to Tabley House

C

PLUMLEY

to Chester

Places of interest
Arley Hall (HHA) – 3m, Tatton Park.(NT) – 2m
Tabley House – 1m

19	Manchester	Macclesfield A556
	Northwich	Knutsford A537

Ⓐ Windmill Inn
Tabley
☎ 01565 631 993
Last orders: 12.00am to 9.00pm daily.
££

A Free House serving traditional Real Ales and
bar meals. It has its own car park and is
opposite a filling station.
Children and dogs
are welcome.

Ⓑ Fryers Nurseries
Nr Knutsford
☎ 01565 750 752
Last orders: 9.00am to 4.30pm.
3.30pm on Sundays.
£

Part of a Garden Centre although run by
different management.
Light meals during the
day when the Garden
Centre is open. Large
car park for caravan
and horseboxes.
Children
welcome but not dogs.

19   Manchester   Macclesfield A556
Northwich   Knutsford A537

C The Smoker *

Plumley
☎ 01565 722 338
Last orders: 2.15pm and 9.15pm.
9.00pm on Sundays.
ff

Named after a race horse bred by the
Prince Regent. It is a traditional pub with a
large garden, a comfortable restaurant,
open fires and plenty of seating. The
building is over 400 years old and is
rumoured to have a ghost, so dogs not
welcome but children
allowed.

29	Preston M65
	Blackburn Burnley M65

Not an easy junction. Turn right at the traffic
lights and bear right at the village green.

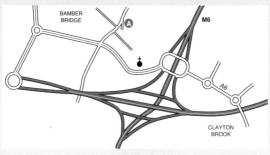

Ⓐ **Ye Olde Hob Inn** ✲

Bamber Bridge
☎ 01772 336 863
Last orders: 2.00pm and 9.00pm.
Closed on Monday evenings.
_££_

A welcome surprise to find an old rustic,
thatch roofed traditional pub, although it
is owned by Scottish and Newcastle. It has
a restaurant as well as a bar, with outside
seating and a family room for wet
weather. Children but no dogs.

31 Preston & Blackburn A59
Clitheroe A59

Keep your head when negotiating the roundabouts on each side of the motorway.

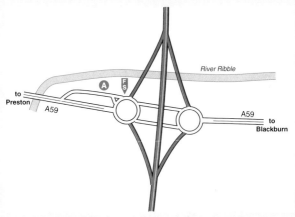

Places of interest
Samlesbury Hall. (Samlesbury Hall Trust) – 2m

 The Tickled Trout Inn
Nr Samlesbury
☎ 01772 877 671
Last orders: 2.00pm and 9.45pm.
££££ 🛏

Now part of the Macdonalds hotel chain, it has 72 bedrooms, conference facilities, a leisure centre and a golf course nearby. For those who would like a bar meal and look at the river, there is outside seating. Children are welcome as are dogs belonging to residents.

Rugby to Carlisle

NORTHERN SECTION 33 to 44

This section is the most scenic of any of the motorways. After Lancaster, which is an interesting county town, the motorway ascends past Kendal, with the the Lake District to the west and the Pennines to the east. Once over Shap, the highest point of the motorway, it descends past Penrith which is a picturesque market town, to Carlisle which is well worth a visit. From there the motorway crosses over the River Esk into Scotland.

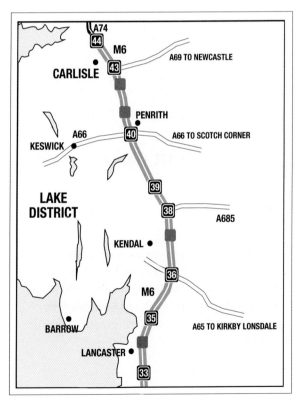

33 Lancaster (S) A6
Garstang   Fleetwood A6

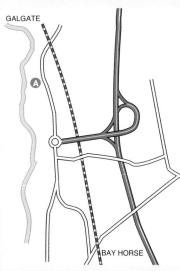

GALGATE

BAY HORSE

Easy enough to
get off the
motorway.

Canalside Craft Centre
Galgate
☎ 01524 752 223
Last orders: 4.00pm.
_ff_

A craft centre with a coffee shop, serving
everything from toast to a full meal. An ideal
spot for those just wanting a light or full lunch
and an airing for dogs or children along the
canal. Home made meals, soups and cakes a
speciality.

35 Morecambe (A6)
Carnforth A601(M)

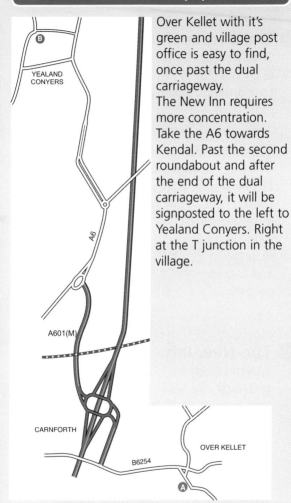

Over Kellet with it's green and village post office is easy to find, once past the dual carriageway.
The New Inn requires more concentration. Take the A6 towards Kendal. Past the second roundabout and after the end of the dual carriageway, it will be signposted to the left to Yealand Conyers. Right at the T junction in the village.

Places of interest
Leighton Hall (HHA) – 3m

35 Morecambe (A6)
Carnforth A601(M)

A The Eagles Head
Over Kellet
☎ 01524 732 457
Last orders: 2.00pm and 9.00pm.
ff

A cheerful country pub owned by Mitchells and
Butler. Bar meals served daily in a large dining
area cum bar with exposed stone walls and
timber ceilings. It specialises in home cured and
cooked ham.
It has a children's
room, outside
seating
and its own
car park.

B The New Inn
Yealand Conyers
☎ 01524 732 938
Last orders: 12.00am to 9.30pm daily
ff

A family run village pub with an
imaginative menu and a friendly
atmosphere. A non smoking dining room
and a bar which also serves bar meals.
Outside seating and a
beer garden. Parking
for cars and
horseboxes. Dogs
and children
allowed.

36 S.Lakes Kendal Barrow A590
Kirkby Lonsdale Skipton A65

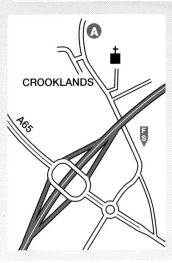

A boring junction with dual carriageways on either side. Look out for the Crookland Hotel signs.

Places of interest
Levens Hall. (HHA) – 4m
Sizergh Castle.(NT) – 4m

Ⓐ Crooklands Hotel *

Crooklands
☎ 01539 567 432
Last orders: 2.00pm and 9.00pm.
£££

A comfortable privately owned hotel with 30 double rooms in a new extension. It has a restaurant as well as a carvery with bars also serving meals. Morning coffee for the passing motorist. Children, but no dogs.

38 Appleby B6260
Kendal   Brough A685

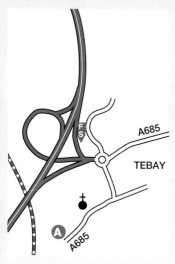

Somewhat complicated with dual carriageways leading off and onto the motorway. After the roundabout, drive through Tebay on the road to Kindal.

Places of interest
The Roman fort and road at Low Borrowbridge. (If you can get to it!) – 3m

Ⓐ **The Cross Keys** ∗
Tebay
☎ 01539 624 240
Last orders: 3.00pm and 9.30pm.
££

A 500 year old coaching inn on the way to Appleby. It is privately owned with a cheerful and friendly staff. It still caters for motorists and has 9 double rooms, outside seating and the best steak and mushroom pies in the area. Children and dogs are welcome. Parking for caravans and horseboxes.

39   Kendal
      Shap (A6)

An easy junction.

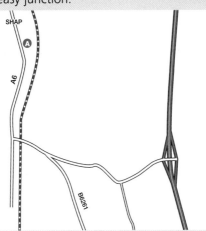

Places of interest
Shap Abbey. (EH) – 3m

Ⓐ The Greyhound Hotel
Shap
☎ 01931 716 4
Last orders: 2.00pm and 9.00pm.
££ 🛏

This was once a coaching inn, built in 1680 where apparently Bonnie Prince Charlie spent a night on his way south, but since then it has been modernised. It serves local lamb and fresh fish from Fleetwood. It has 11 bedrooms, but beware of the main railway line just behind. Children and dogs allowed. Parking for caravan and horseboxes.

40 N. Lakes Keswick Penrith A66
Brough A66

A busy junction with traffic coming in from the
Lake District or going to Scotch Corner. Penrith
was once the crossing point for the coaching
traffic going north and south and also for those
going to the Cumbrian ports or over the Pennines
to Barnard Castle. As a result there is a plethora
of old coaching inns and wayside pubs to this
day.
The Red Rooster Roadstop, part of the garage at
the first roundabout in Penrith does a good
breakfast for lorry drivers and others.

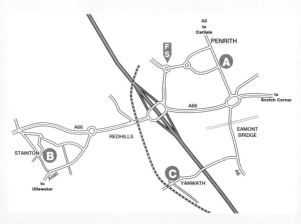

Places of interest
Dalemain (HHA) – 2½m
Penrith Castle.
The Toffee Shop, Penrith.
King Arthur's Round Table (EH) – 1m
Mayburgh Henge (EH) – 1m
Hutton in the Forest (HHA) – 7m

> **40** N. Lakes Keswick Penrith A66
> Brough A66

Ⓐ The George Hotel

Penrith

☎ 01768 862 696

Last orders: 2.30pm and 10.00pm.
9.30 on Sundays, during the winter.

£££ 🛏

A privately owned hotel in the centre of
Penrith which has been a coaching inn for
the past 300 years. It is a fast disappearing
example of old style comfort and service.
It has been recently refurbished and has
34 bedrooms, a restaurant and a bar. The
carpark at the rear, where the carriages
used to be, is locked at
nights. Children are
permitted and dogs at a
charge. You can still order
afternoon tea with scones
and toasted teacakes by
pressing a bell.

Ⓑ Brantwood Country Hotel

Stainton

☎ 01768 862 748

Last orders: 2.00pm and 8.45pm.

££ 🛏

A family owned hotel and restaurant with
7 bedrooms and a large garden. A 19th
century comfortably
furnished house
with a
restaurant,
oak beams
and log fires.

40   N. Lakes   Keswick   Penrith A66
Brough A66

C The Yanwath Gate Inn

Yanwath
☎ 01768 862 386
Last orders: 2.15pm to 9.30pm.
9.00pm on Sundays.
££

A privately owned pub dating from 1683 in a
quiet secluded lane. It has a restaurant and bar,
as well as outside seating. Dogs and children
allowed. The sign over the door says "This gate
hangs well and hinders none. Refresh and pay
and travel on". It has recently changed hands.

43	Carlisle
	Hexham Newcastle A69

After coming off the junction there is a stretch of
dual carriageway at the end of which is the
Waterloo.
For the Queen's Arms Hotel continue on towards
Warwick on Eden and take a slip road to the right.
If you come to the traffic lights on the bridge over
the river Eden you have gone too far.

Places of interest
*Carlisle, with its Castle and Norman Cathedral – 2m;
Wetheral Priory Gatehouse – 3m; Corby Castle – 2m*

 # The Waterloo
Aglionby
☎ 01228 513 347
Last orders: 2.30pm and 8.45pm.
££

A small traditional wayside pub serving bar
meals. It has a beer garden
and a car park at rear.
Yes to children,
but no to dogs.

43 Carlisle
Hexham　Newcastle　A69

Ⓑ **Queen's Arms Hotel**　　*
Warwick on Eden
☎ 01228 560 699
Last orders: 1.45pm and 8.45pm.
Closed for Monday lunches
££　🛏

The house was converted into a pub in the
19th Century. It is a pleasant and friendly place
with 6 bedrooms, a restaurant with a good
menu specialising in fish and a bar as well as a
lounge. Children allowed indoors but dogs
outside only.

> **44** Carlisle
> Galashiels   Hawick A7

The end of the M6 as a motorway, but it continues as the dual carriageway A74 over the Border where it becomes the A74(M). To get back from the Wallfoot Hotel (which is just five minutes) you will have to retrace your way back to Junction 44.

Places of interest
Hadrian's Wall.

Ⓐ Wallfoot Hotel & Restaurant
Crosby on Eden
☎ 01228 573 696
Last Orders: 2.00pm and 9.00pm No lunches on Mondays and Tuesdays. Breakfast.
££ 🛏

A small privately owned hotel with 7 bedrooms, a comfortable restaurant and a bar where lounge meals are served. Dogs and children permitted in the garden at rear. Breakfast for the passing motorist.

44	Carlisle
	Galashiels Hawick A7

Both the Castleton Farm Shop and the Metal Bridge Inn are on the No Mans Land of the A74 between Scotland and England. Keep an eye out for the sign off the A74 saying Rockcliffe and Castletown for the Farm Shop.

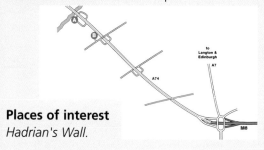

Places of interest
Hadrian's Wall.

 # Metal Bridge Inn
Blackford
☎ 01228 674 044
Last orders: 2.00pm and 9.00pm.
£   🍴

Once an old coaching inn, it is four miles beyond Junction 44, on the banks of the River Esk just before the Scottish Border. It is privately owned and has 5 bedrooms. Bar meals are available in the dining areas. Children and dogs welcome.

44 | Carlisle
Galashiels   Hawick A7

B Castleton Farm Shop
Rockclife
☎ 01228 674 400
Last orders: 9.30pm to 4.00pm.
££ 🍸

A family business selling its own farm produce and other delicacies. It serves breakfast, light lunches and afternoon tea for the passing motorist and offers the chance to purchase a last minute present for prospective guests on their way north. Children allowed but dogs outside. The sharp turning into the car park could be a hazard for horseboxes.

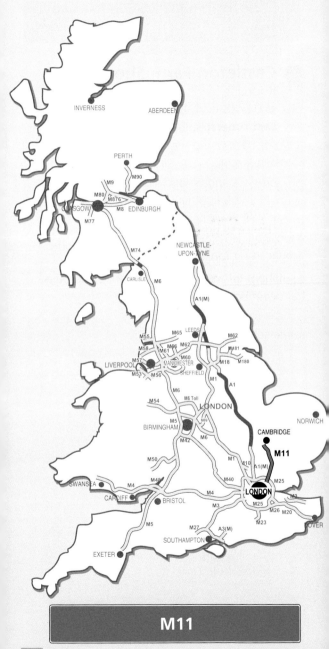

M11

London to Cambridge

Junctions 7 to 14

For those travelling to or from the south and the Channel Tunnel it is a good alternative to the M1 as it links the M25 with the A1(M) at Huntingdon.

The southern section goes past the newish town of Harlow and the congestion around Stansted Airport.

Once north of them, the countryside is pleasant enough and passes some attractive towns such as Saffron Walden and the imposing pile of Audley End. At Duxford is the American Air Museum.

Cambridge of course is a must for anyone who has never been there.

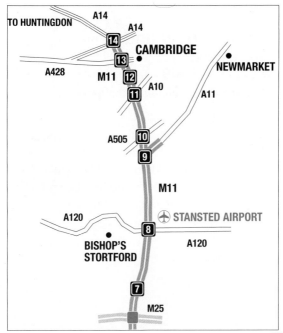

7 | Harlow A414 Chelmsford

The roundabout is controlled by lights. Take the Chelmsford road and almost immediately turn off to the left on a small road which is marked St Clare Hospice and Hastingwood.

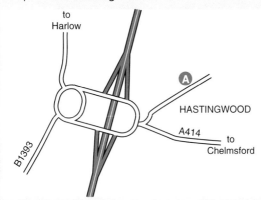

Ⓐ **The Rainbow and Dove**
Hastingwood
☎ 01279 415 419
Last orders: 2.30pm and 9.30pm.
££

Said to date from the 15th century, it was a pub by 1640 when Cromwell's soldiers stopped to slake their thirst. There is outside seating in a garden and inside a roaring fire during the winter. Children discouraged, but dogs allowed in the grounds.

London to Cambridge

8 Stansted Airport Colchester Bishop's Stortford A120

Construction work has been completed to cope with the increasing traffic to and from Stansted Airport. Keep going round the roundabout until you see the small turnoff for Birchanger.

A The Three Willows ∗
Birchanger
☎ 01279 815 913
Last orders: 2.00pm and 9.00pm.
No evening meals on Sundays.
££

A popular country pub with an interest in cricket, judging by the sign and inside, part has been designated The Oval. Bar meals specialising in fish. Children's playground, where they are encouraged to stay.
No dogs.

9   Newmarket   Norwich A11

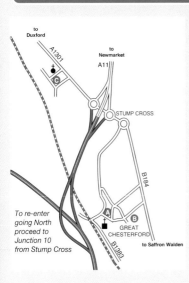

This junction gives direct access to the Newmarket road. Turn off where marked Great Chesterford before crossing over the road. If driving north, you must access again at Junction 10 and vice versa.

Places of interest
Audley End (EH) – 5m
Saffron Walden – 6m

The Crown House Hotel
Great Chesterford
☎ 01799 530 515
Last orders: 9.00pm including Sundays.
£££

There has been a building on the site since Roman times. The foundations of the present one date from 1560. It is a privately owned hotel with modern stone flagged floors, 22 bedrooms, a restaurant and a bar serving barmeals. Dogs and children are provided for.

9   Newmarket   Norwich A11

ⒷThe Plough
Great Chesterford
☎ 01799 530 283
Last orders: 2.30pm and 8.30pm.
8.00pm Sunday evenings. No evening
meals on Mondays.
_££_

A friendly village pub for 200 years owned
by Greene King. It has a modern restaurant
and bar serving Real Ales. Large children's
playground and
family room.
Outside seating
where children
and dogs are
welcome. Facilities for the disabled.

ⒸThe Red Lion
Hinxton
☎ 01799 530 601
Last orders: 1.45pm and 9.45pm
including Sundays.
_£££_

A 16th century pub in this attractive village.
A well deserved reputation for home
cooking in the
restaurant and bar.
Dogs and children
permitted in the
garden. It has
recently changed
hands

> ### 10   Duxford   Royston A505
> ### Saffron Walden A1301

Turn left off the Newmarket road to Whittlesford village as opposed to the station. Past the village green and sharp left and right. The Tickell Arms is on the left.

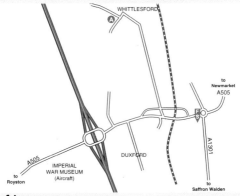

Places of interest
The Imperial War Museum – ½ mile
and American Air Museum.

B The Tickell Arms
Whittlesford
☎ 01223 833 128
Last orders: 2.00pm and 9.00pm. On Sunday
2.30pm. Closed Mondays.
£££

The Tickell Arms is now a restaurant with a bar.
The chef was trained by Pierre White so it is
not for those in a rush as it would be a pity not
to be able to relax in comfortable surroundings
complete with candles and log fires.
Children allowed at
weekend but no
dogs. A water
garden at the rear.

11 Cambridge A1309
Royston   Harston A10

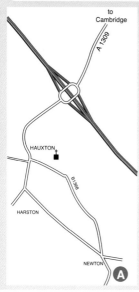

From the junction take the A10 to Royston. After about half a mile turn left onto the B1368 to Newton. The Queen's Head is on the other side of the village green

Places of interest
Docwra's Manor – 5m
Willers Mill – 5m

Ⓐ **Queens Head** ＊
Newton
☎ 01223 870 436
Last orders: 2.30pm and 9.30pm every day.
£££

Pleasant and friendly with well furnished dining alcoves and bars and a host of interesting mementoes. It is more than typical of the traditional English
pub and restaurant.
Children
welcome and
dogs outside.

12 Cambridge A603
Sandy

Do not be too put off by the modern development in Barton. The picturesque village of Grantchester is easy to find, which was made famous by the First World War poet Rupert Brooke, "....Is there honey still for tea?"

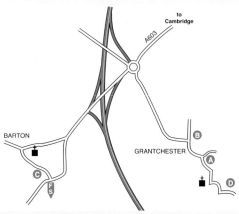

Places of interest
Wimpole Hall (NT) – 6m

Ⓐ The Green Man
Grantchester
☎ 01223 841 178
Last orders: 3.00pm and 9.00pm.
££

A simple pub in the centre of the village which has been renovated with wooden floors and a bar. Extensive car park at the rear. Children and dogs allowed in the garden.

12 Cambridge A603
Sandy

B The Rupert Brooke
Grantchester
☎ 01223 840 295
Last orders: 2.30pm and 9.30pm.
£££

Converted from a 19th century house, into a
privately owned pub which is folksy but
cheerful, complete with beams.
There is outside seating at the front and a
patio and garden at the rear, overlooking the
meadows. Children
over 14 but
no dogs
or coaches.

C The White Horse
Barton
☎ 01223 262 327
Last orders: 12.00pm to 9.00pm.
8.00pm on Sundays
££

A welcoming 400 year old pub, owned by
Greene King. It has a restaurant, and two
bars, as well as five bedrooms. Outside there
is a beer garden
and a car park for
horseboxes
and caravans.
Children and
dogs are
allowed.

Ⓓ **The Orchard** ✳
Grantchester
☎ 01223 845 788
Last orders: 10.30pm to 6.30pm.
£££

Now over 100 years old it is still an old
fashioned tearoom complete with 1920s
deckchairs, punts and nostalgia. You almost
expect to see previous visitors such as Rupert
Brooke, Virgina Woolf, A.A. Milne or John
Betjeman appear from behind an apple tree.
There are light lunches available as well as
traditional teas indoors and out depending on
the weather.
Children and well trained dogs are welcome.

13/14 Cambridge A1303 Ely (A10)
Bedford (A428) Newmarket A14

Junction 13 is easy for those coming from the
south, but Junction 14, for those from the North
will require a Degree in map reading. However
well worth the effort to get to Madingley.

**Places
of
interest**
*Madingley Hall.
American Military Cemetary*

 The Three Horseshoes *

Madingley

☎ 01954 210 221

Last orders: 2.00pm and 9.00pm.
On Sunday evenings Bar Grills are
available.

££££

Part of a small group of well managed
pub/restaurants run by chefs. It is efficient
and smart. Inside there is a restaurant and
long bar, with a conservatory
at the rear. Outside there
is a pleasant garden.

Junctions 1 to 6

This 30 mile motorway was built to link the M1 to the A1(M) at Doncaster, then with the M180 spur to Grimsby and finally with the M62 Trans Pennine near Goole. It is a useful linking motorway, as you can switch from the M1 or else cut off a corner when travelling from or to Hull. That being said the countryside is flat and uninteresting.

Selby however, to the north of the intersection with the M62, is worth a visit as the abbey was built at the same time and probably by the same masons as Durham Cathedral.

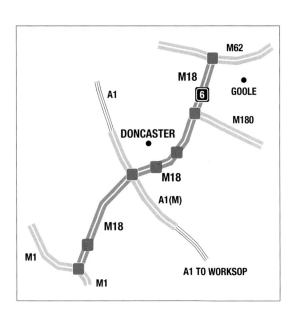

6   Thorne A614

This is an area of low fen land and irrigation ditches. The Waterside, where canal boats once disgorged their cargoes, was renowned for having seven pubs but only one now remains. It is said that an Elizabethan warship was built here to harass the Armada.

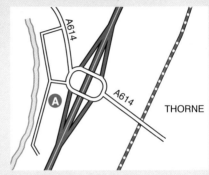

A614

A614

THORNE

Places of interest

The birthplace of Thomas Crapper, the manufacturer of flushing lavatories.

Ⓐ The John Bull Inn

Waterside
☎ 01405 814 677
Last orders: 2.30pm and 9.30pm.
££

A traditional inn, by the canal, where ale has been served to thirsty bargemen since the 1500s. It has a restaurant which is used in the evening but otherwise serves bar meals. Children and dogs are welcome.

M20

London to Folkestone

Junctions **1** to **13**

The M20 is 40 miles long and was started in 1961 and finished twenty years later. It is the main motorway from the Channel Ports to link up directly with the M25 and the motorway system.

It goes through some very attractive scenery, being the Garden of Kent and it should be enjoyed before it is engulfed with proposals to submerge it with new houses around Ashford. After Maidstone with its orchards and oast houses, the M20 climbs the shoulder of the North Weald on its way to London, whilst the M26 spur continues and links up with the southern segment of the M25.

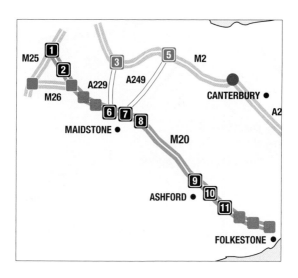

1 Swanley B2173
Dartford Crossing M25

It is not so complicated as it may appear. On the motorway roundabout it will be signed Farningham A20. Do not be put off by passing the Highways Recycling Centre. Turn right at the roundabout by the filling station. It is still a surprisingly attractive rural village although so near to London.

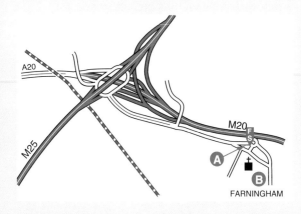

Places of interest
Eynsford Castle. (EH) – 2m
Lullingstone Roman Villa (EH) – 3m

1 Swanley B2173
Dartford Crossing M25

Ⓐ The Chequers
Farningham
☎ 01322 865 222
Last orders: 2.30pm.
£

A simple local pub serving bar meals at lunch only with home made pies, sandwiches and a range of beers and stout. Some seating outside on the pavement and dogs are welcome. Street parking only.

Ⓑ Pied Bull
Farningham
☎ 01322 862 125
Last orders: 2.00pm and 8.45pm No evening meals on Sundays. Closed Mondays.
££

It was known as The Bull in 1612. It has recently been fully modernised and produces bar meals, especially steak and kidney pies. Dogs and children under control welcomed in the enclosed garden.

Paddock Wood Gravesend Tonbridge (A22) Wrotham

Junction 2 is in reality two exits joined by a normal road. Coming from London it is easy enough to get off at the first exit to get to Wrotham, which is a picturesque village. You must then rejoin by driving to Junction 2a on the M26 which joins the M20 a mile further on! It is not as bad as it sounds. The converse is true for those driving from the Channel Tunnel.

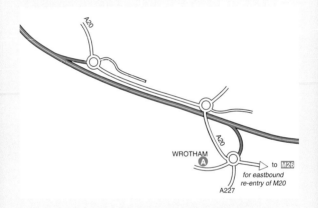

Places of interest
Brands Hatch Racing Circuit – 3m

**Paddock Wood Gravesend
Tonbridge (A22) Wrotham**

 ## Bull Hotel
Wrotham
☎ 01732 789 800
Last orders: 2.00pm and 9.45pm
9.30pm on Sundays.
£££   🛏

A listed Georgian house but dating from
the 14th century. It has recently changed
hands and been refurbished. Fresh local
food in the restaurant and lounge bar.
Outside seating. Morning coffee for the
passing motorist. For the overnight guests
there are 12 bedrooms.Children and dogs
allowed.

There have been road improvements to the A229 which has made it easier to reach the two places mentioned.

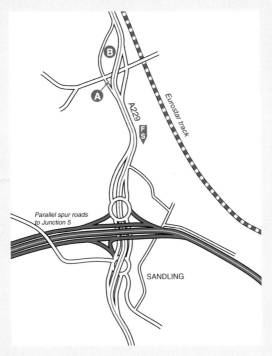

Places of interest
*Kits Coty,
prehistoric burial mound
Museum of Kent Life.*

London to Folkestone

6 Maidstone A20
Chatham A229

Ⓐ Lower Bell
Blue Bell Hill
☎ 01634 861 127
Last orders: 2.45pm and 9.45pm.
_ff_

The word Lower in the name is appropriate as
it is now surrounded by high embankments of
the new road layout. These do not detract
from the warm welcome and choice of four
Real Ales with the
bar meals.
There is some
outside seating
at the rear where
dogs are allowed.

Ⓑ Kits Coty Brasserie
Kits Coty
☎ 01634 684 445
Last orders: 2.00pm and 9.00pm.
Closed Sunday evenings.
_ff_

A family run brasserie for the past seventeen
years. It has sweeping views south over
Maidstone and the Weald. A well kept
garden enhances its surroundings. Modern art
deco furnishing with glass and chrome.

7 Canterbury Ramsgate A249
Maidstone Sheerness

This junction is close to Maidstone and therefore it is a more built up area. The new Eurostar railtrack makes it more confusing.

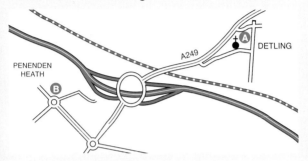

Ⓐ The Cock Horse Inn
Detling
☎ 01622 737 092
Last orders: From 11.00am to 10.00pm.
9.30pm on Sundays.
££

A refurbished 15th c coaching inn in the middle of this rural village well accessed by new roads. It has a beamed non-smoking restaurant and bar, where imaginative home cooking is served and coffee all day. A secluded garden at the rear. Dogs and children are welcome.

The Chiltern Hundreds
Penenden Heath
☎ 01622 752 335
Last orders: 10.00pm. 9.30pm on
Sundays.
£££

It has been a coaching stop since 1830.
Why it should give the impression of giving
an MP the chance to leave Parliament in a
hurry is not known. It is part of the Chef
and Brewer chain, so now has open areas
serving bar meals from 11am. Some
outside seating and a large carpark.
Facilities for the disabled. Dogs not
welcome. A comfort stop.

8　Lenham A20　Maidstone

Not a complicated junction but look out for the
sign to Hollingbourne

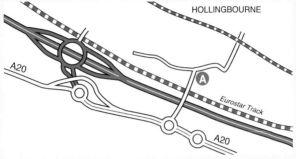

HOLLINGBOURNE

A20

Eurostar Track

A20

Places of interest
Leeds Castle. (HHA) Stoneacre. (NT) – 1m

 The Windmill　*

Hollingbourne
☎ 01622 880 280
Last orders: 2.30pm and 10.00pm.
9.30pm on Sundays.
££

A privately owned pub in an attractive village,
which dates back partially to the 16th Century.
It has a restaurant and bar with home cooked
meals. Outside there is a new playground and
a beer garden at the rear, with seating in front.
The resident dog takes priority over all canine
visitors so check beforehand.

9 Ashford A20 Canterbury (A28)
Tenterden Faversham (A251)

A modern junction and road system, which does not seem to bode well in finding anything suitable, but persist.

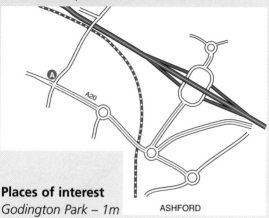

Places of interest
Godington Park – 1m

ASHFORD

 # Hare and Hounds
Potters Corner
☎ 01233 621 760
Last orders: 2.30pm and 9.30pm.
Closed Monday evenings.
££

Once an 18th century inn, it has been modernised, but still retains character and serves Real Ales. The road outside is busy but there is some
outside
seating.

10 Ashford A292
Brenzett A2070

A built up area, not helped by a large Tesco just off the Motorway. The pub is pleasant enough when you reach it but you may prefer to drive on.

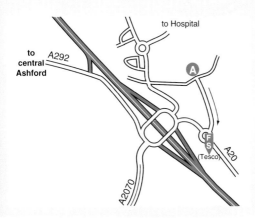

Ⓐ Blacksmiths Arms

Willesborough Green
☎ 01233 623 975
Last orders: 2.30pm and 9.00pm.
9.00pm on Sundays.
££

Some 300 years old and probably the old smithy, the forge is now replaced by log fires and the heat reduced by pints of Real Ale, in either the beamed restaurant or the bar. There is a large garden at the rear where dogs are welcome. One Armed Bandits for the bored.

> **11** Canterbury B 2068
> Hastings A259   Hythe A261

The new Eurostar track now runs alongside the
motorway. Circle round to the north on the B
2068 and the pub can be seen on the left.

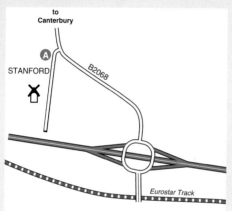

The Drum
Stanford
☎ 01303 812 125
Last orders: 2.30pm and 9.00pm.
££

It is the last pub before (or first after) the
Tunnel. It has been a country pub for some
200 years. Log fires still burn in the grates.
There is a restaurant and a bar for snacks
and Real Ales. Outside seating in the
garden. Dogs welcome. Sunday Roasts
are their speciality.

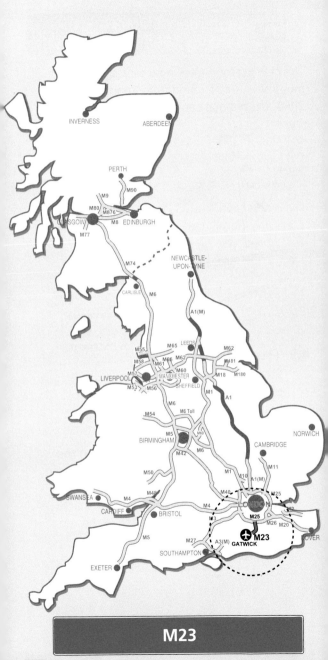

M23

Caterham to Crawley

Junctions   7   to   11

Built to give quick access from Gatwick Airport to London, this 18 mile stretch took nearly four years to complete. However, the roads south of Croydon are such that many motorists prefer to head west out of London to link up with the M25 and then drive round to the M23.

Gatwick Airport started life as a racecourse in the 19th century before becoming one of the busiest airports in the UK in spite of only having one runway.

At Junction 11 it continues as the A23 to Brighton.

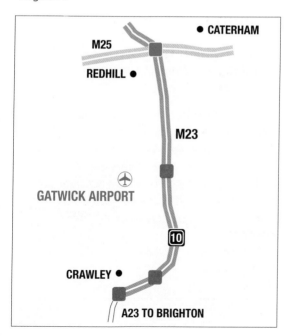

> **10**   Crawley
> East Grinstead A264

An easy junction and the Hotel is on the other side of the roundabout.

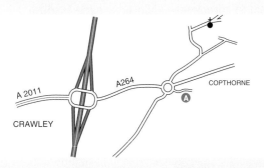

Places of interest
Wakehurst Place (NT) – 8m

Ⓐ Copthorne Hotel

Copthorne
☎ 01342 714 971
Last orders: 2.00pm and 10.45pm.
££££

It started life in the 16th century, but has grown out of all proportion since then. Today the White Swan with bar meals is all that is left of that age. Elsewhere there are 227 bedrooms, full range of leisure activities and two restaurants. It is geared for the business community and conferences, but still has time to give a welcome to the passing motorist.

London Orbital

The idea of an orbital ring road round London was first mooted in 1905. The North Circular Road was built in the 1930s but the South Circular exists in name only.

In 1975 a decision was made to construct an integrated Orbital Ring Road which was finally completed in 1986. It was originally intended to have more lanes but this was deemed to be too expensive. It will now cost a fortune to upgrade to cope with the increase in traffic.

The M25 does however make it easier for visitors from abroad to skirt around London and head north or west.

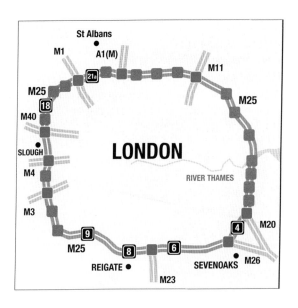

| 4 | **Bromley A21 London**
Orpington (A224) |

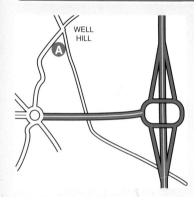

As a junction it is an easy one but at the roundabout look out for a narrow lane signed Well Hill.

Places of interest
Lullingstone – 2m
Roman VIlla (EH) Lullingstone Castle(HHA) – 2m

 Bo Peep Restaurant *

Well Hill
☎ 01959 534 457
Last orders: 2.00pm and 9.45pm.
No evening meals on Sundays.
££

It has been an alehouse since 1549. It is a surprise to find it so close to London and in the middle of strawberry fields.
It has a non smoking restaurant and a bar for snacks.
A well kept garden and inside, a friendly welcome.

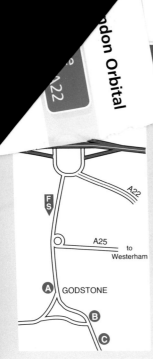

(A25) Eastbourne
dstone A22

his should not be any
trouble but do not take
the dual carriageway.
Godstone is an attractive
place, surrounding a
village green.

Places of interest
Chartwell (NT) – 8m
Squerryes Court (HHA) – 7m
Quebec House – 7m

Ⓐ The Hare and Hounds
Godstone
☎ 01883 742 296
Last orders: 3.00pm and 9.00pm.
9.00pm on Sundays.
££

A traditional English village pub, with beamed
eating areas. There is some outside seating
under a spreading chestnut tree. Children and
dogs are not encouraged, but inside there is a
friendly welcome.

Ⓑ The White Hart

Godstone
☎ 01883 742 521
Last orders: 2.30pm and 10.30pm
9pm on Sundays.
££

According to the blurb, it was established in
the reign of Richard II and enlarged at the time
of Good Queen Bess. It is now part of the
Beefeater chain and therefore somewhat
standardised. It is still a cheerful place with
original beams, log fires and efficient service.
There is outside seating and a car park.

6 Westerham   Eastbourne
Redhill (A25)   Godstone A22

C Coach House Restaurant and Godstone Hotel

Godstone

☎ 01883 742 461

Last orders: 2.00pm and 10.00pm.
9.00pm on Sundays

£££

A comfortable friendly family run hotel with a bar. It is some 400 years old, but apparently not as old as the willow tree in the garden. For those wishing to stay, after tasting one of their flambéed specialities at dinner in the Coach House Restaurant, there are 8 double bedrooms available.

| 8 | Sutton   Reigate A217
Leatherhead A243 Dorking (A24) |

Keep a look-out after the roundabout as you might easily miss the turning. If you do, carry on to the crossroads.

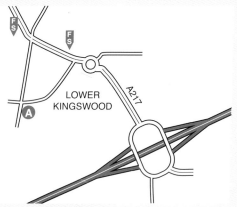

Ⓐ **Mint Arms**
Lower Kingswood
☎ 01737 242 957
Last orders: 3pm and 10.00pm.
9.30pm on Sundays.
£££

A Free House tucked away in a small village. It does have a restaurant as well as the usual bars for meals. Outside there is a playground, a beer garden where they have Barbecues, weather permitting and dogs
and children are allowed.
A pool table and
dart board for
wet days.

9 Kingston A243
Leatherhead   Dorking A24

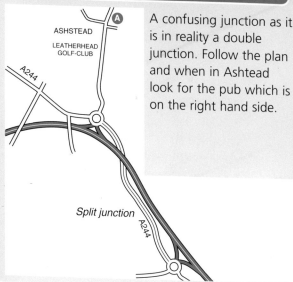

ASHSTEAD

LEATHERHEAD
GOLF-CLUB

A244

A

Split junction A244

A confusing junction as it is in reality a double junction. Follow the plan and when in Ashtead look for the pub which is on the right hand side.

A Leg of Mutton and Cauliflower (LOMAC)

Ashstead

☎ 01372 277 200

Last orders: 3.00pm and 10.00pm. 8.00pm on Sundays.

£££

A franchised pub which specialises in fish. From outside it is not inspiring. However, walk through and there is a modern comfortable restaurant with a well laid out garden at the rear. Children welcome.

**18 Rickmansworth A404
Chorleywood Amersham**

An easy junction but at the cross roads look out for Dog Kennel Road.

Places of interest
Chenies Manor House – 3m

Ⓐ **The Black Horse ＊**
Chorleywood Common
☎ 01923 282 252
Last orders: 2.15pm and 9.15pm.
8.00pm on Sundays.
£££

This could be deep in the countryside instead of being just off the motorway. It has been a pub since the early 1800s and still produces home cooked specials by log fires. There is seating at the front and a beer garden at the rear. Children are welcome and dogs. The car park can take horseboxes.

London Orbital

21a St Albans A405
Watford Harrow

This looks a a complicated junction but you just
follow the signs.

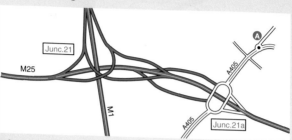

Places of interest
St Albans Abbey – 3m
Verulanium Roman City – 2m

 ## Thistle St Albans
Chiswell Green
☎ 01727 854 252
Last orders: 2.00pm and 7.00pm. (in the
Brasserie)
9pm on Sundays.
££££ 🛏

This hotel is not for the casual passer-by, as it
sets a high standard in comfort and price.
There are 111 bedrooms supported by every
form of comfort and relaxation, such as a
swimming pool, gym and a sauna. There is a
restaurant, carvery and bars. Children are
welcomed
and dogs
by prior
arrangement.

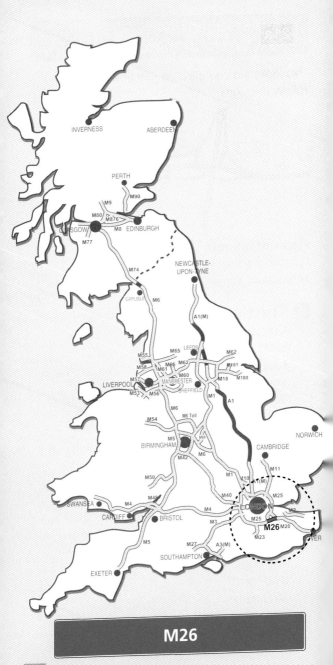

INVERNESS

ABERDEEN

PERTH

M9

M90

M80
M876
GLASGOW
M8   EDINBURGH
M77

M74

NEWCASTLE-
UPON-TYNE

CARLISLE   M6

A1(M)

M55   LEEDS   M62
M65
M66   M62
M58   M61   M181
M57   M60   M18   M180
LIVERPOOL   MANCHESTER
M53   M56   SHEFFIELD
M6   M1   A1

M54   M6 Toll

M5   M69
BIRMINGHAM

M42   M6

M50   M1   M11
M40   M10   A1(M)
CAMBRIDGE

NORWICH

SWANSEA   M4   M48   LONDON   M25
CARDIFF   M4   M25   M2
BRISTOL   M3   **M26** M20
M23   DOVER
M5   M27   A3(M)
SOUTHAMPTON
EXETER

M26

2a Borough Green Maidstone A25 Gravesend A227

An 8 mile stretch of motorway, built in 1980, to form a link from the M20 with the southern segment of the M25.

Useful for those who have misread the M20 signs and find themselves on the M26 going west, as they can rejoin the M20 at Junction 2a to Wrotham.

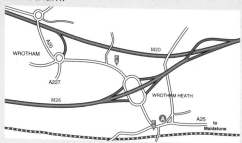

Places of interest

Old Soar Manor (EH) – 3m
Ightam Mote. (NT) – 5m
St Leonards Tower. (EH) – 4m

 ## The Vineyard

Wrotham Heath
☎ 01732 882 330
Last orders: 2.30pm and 10.30pm.
£££

A family run restaurant, specialising in sea food with French and Italian cooking. Although on the road, it is surrounded by a secluded garden and private car park. Small and friendly. Children allowed but no dogs.

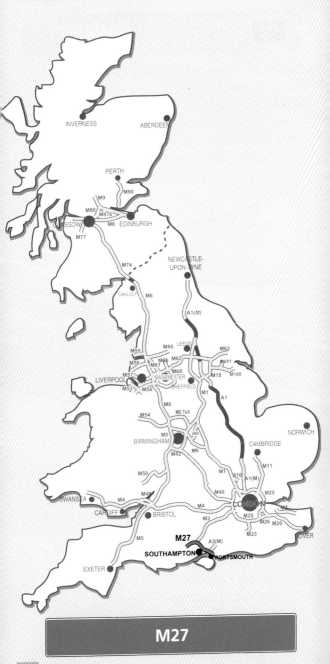

INVERNESS

ABERDEEN

PERTH

M90
M9
M80
M876
M8 EDINBURGH
GLASGOW
M77
M74

NEWCASTLE-UPON-TYNE

CARLISLE
M6

A1(M)

M55
M58
M57
LIVERPOOL
M53
M56
M65 LEEDS
M66
M61
M62
M60
MANCHESTER
SHEFFIELD
M1
A1
M62
M181
M18
M180

M6

M54
M6 Toll
M5
M6
BIRMINGHAM
M42
M60
M6

M50
M1
A10
A1(M)
M40
M25
M4
M48
M4
LONDON
M25
M3
M26 M20
M23

NORWICH

CAMBRIDGE

M11

DOVER

SWANSEA
CARDIFF
BRISTOL

M5

M27
A3(M)
SOUTHAMPTON PORTSMOUTH

EXETER

M27

New Forest to Portsmouth   M27

The M27, 27 miles long, was built to connect Portsmouth and Southampton with the M3. It starts or ends rather abruptly at the edge of the New Forest, but continues as a dual carriageway nearly as far as Bournemouth. At the Portsmouth end it joins up with the A3(M) before carrying on as a dual-carriageway to Chichester, Brighton and Lewes (with some breaks). It is conceivable that one day there could be a motorway along the south coast to Dover. This would help alleviate the plight of foreign visitors who at present have to head for London and the M25, whatever their destination.

1 Lyndhurst
Cadnam A337

Once off the junction, you might miss the sign to
the Sir John Barleycorn on your left. To the north
of the junction, the road will take you into the
New Forest proper, but you will not get lost.

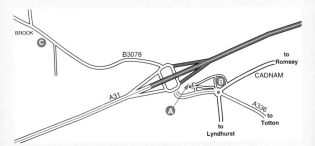

Places of interest
*The Rufus Stone – 1m; Hamptworth Lodge (HHA) –
8m; Broadlands House (HHA) – 7m; Paulton's Park
– 3m; Newhouse, Redlynch.(HHA) – 7m*

Ⓐ Sir John Barleycorn
Cadnam
☎ 02380 812 236
Last orders: 9.30pm. 9.00pm on Sundays.
££

The original cottage was the home of a
charcoal burner who discovered the murdered
body of King William Rufus in 1100. It is now a
busy pub which has recently been bought out
by Alcatraz who have refurbished it inside and
out.
Dogs are
allowed in
the beer
garden.

1 Lyndhurst
Cadnam A337

B ## The White Hart ∗
Cadnam
☎ 02380 812 277
Last orders: 2pm and 9.30pm
9pm on Sundays.
£££

A Coaching Inn since the 17th century, it still
gives warm hospitality with log fires and a
profusion of hanging baskets.
Home cooking,
specialising in fish.
There is a playground
and a secluded garden
where dogs are allowed.

C ## The Green Dragon
Brook
☎ 02380 813 359
Last orders: 2.00pm and 9.30pm.
9.00pm on Sundays.
£££

A Whitbread owned pub. It has been a
beerhouse for 200 years, before which it
was used by a coffin maker and before him
by a wheelwright. No sign of the coffin
maker is now apparent,
only a busy,
cheerful atmosphere
in the large bar
for eating.

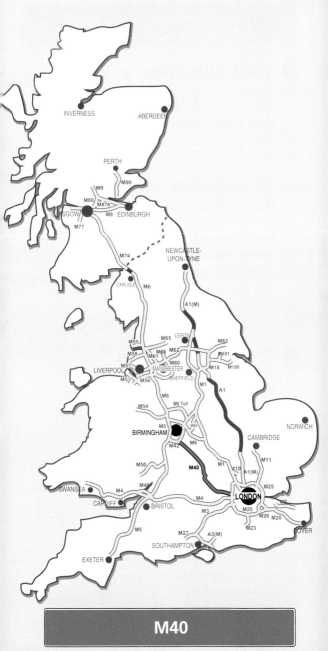

M40

London to Birmingham

Junctions 2 to 16

The first section to Oxford was completed in 1976 but it took fifteen years to link it to the M42. It was completed in 1991 to take the pressure off the M1, to such an extent that now it is almost as crowded.

Beware of Junction 15 with five roads converging on the roundabout as there could be a delay to get to Coventry.

Chesterton Windmill is a prominent landmark on the high ground to the east of the motorway, north of Junction12.

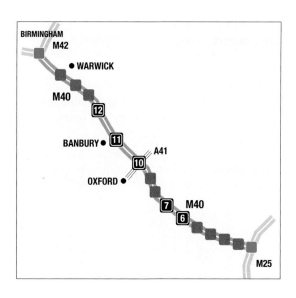

| 6 | Watlington　Thame
Princes Risborough B4009 |

The road to Lewknor can be easily missed, so look out for the sign on the right. The village itself is attractive.

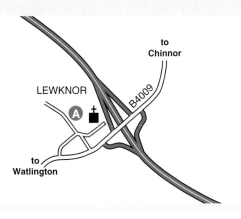

Ⓐ Ye Olde Leather Bottel ✶

Lewknor

☎ 01844 351 482

Last orders: 2.00pm and 9.30pm.

££

Ye Olde Leather Bottel is 450 years old, which makes for a congenial and friendly atmosphere. It specialises in home cooking and serves morning coffee as well as Brakspear Traditional Ales. There is plenty of outside seating in a large garden. Children and dogs welcome.

7 Wallingford A329
Thame

Coming from London there is no difficulty in exiting but returning to the motorway you will have to cross over it, take the A40 and (A418) to Oxford and join up with the motorway at Junction 8A. Coming from the north take the A418 signed Aylesbury and Thame and then the A40 and the A379 to Wallingford.

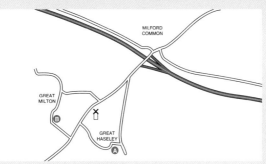

Places of interest *Rycote Chapel 1/2 mile*

Ⓐ **The Plough** *
Great Haseley
☎ 01844 279 283
Last orders: 2.00pm and 10.00pm every day
£££

A thatched roofed pub in the centre of a pleasant rural village. It has recently been taken over and extensive remodelling has been taking place internally. Outside seating and gravel car park. Children and dogs are welcome.

7 Wallingford A329
Thame

Ⓑ Le Manoir aux Quat' Saisons ✳

Great Milton
☎ 01844 278 881
Last orders: 2.30pm and 9.30pm.
£££££ 🛏 🍷

This must be the most famous restaurant in the country.
It is in an old-fashioned setting with a large well kept garden.
There are 32 bedrooms, three restaurant and a conservatory.
Children accepted but dogs outside.
An experience in every sense of the word.

10 Northampton A43
Middleton Stoney B4030

A simple junction off the motorway on to the old road between Oxford and Brackley.

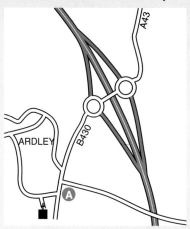

Ⓐ Fox and Hounds
Ardley
☎ 01869 346 883
Last orders: 2.15pm and 9.00pm.
Closed on Sunday evenings.
££

Now owned by an ex-mariner, this 18th Century pub serves traditional ales and a selection of bar meals. Outside seating at the rear and its own car parking.
Children are welcome, as are ex-servicemen who served nearby.

11 Banbury A422

This is the junction for Banbury. Take the A422 to Brackley and after half a mile take the second left at the roundabout signed Middleton Cheney.

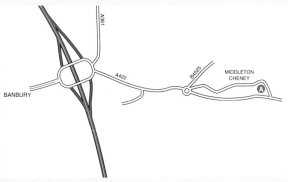

Ⓐ New Inn
Middleton Cheney
☎ 01295 719 399
Last orders: 2.00pm and 9.00pm.
No evening meals on Sundays
££

A tenanted pub of Bass, but it has a traditional and friendly atmosphere with flagstoned floors, serving bar meals.
A beer garden where children and dogs are welcome.

12 Gaydon B4451

Turn left when you get to the A41 and the pub will be signed on your right hand side.

Places of interest

Heritage Motor Museum – 1m
Edgehill Battlefield.1642 – 4m
Upton House (NT) – 9m

A The Malt Shovel Inn *

Gaydon
☎ 01926 641 221
Last orders: 2.00pm and 9.00pm.
seven days a week
£££

A deservedly popular village inn with a bar and a restaurant area.
The owners who used to run auberges and hotels in France are proud to provide real food with real ale.
Dogs and children are welcome provided they behave
themselves.

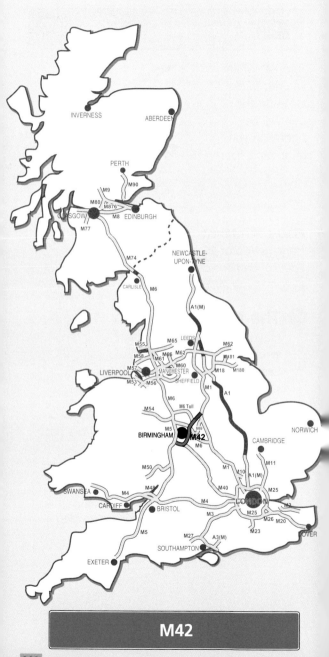

M42

Bromsgrove to Tamworth

Junctions   2 to 11

Completed in 1986, it might be continued as a motorway to join up with the M1 at Nottingham. It is in effect the southern and eastern part of the Birmingham Ring Road, with the M6 and the M5 completing the circuit. It is a useful linkage for those using the M40 from and to the north and also for those who are hoping to avoid the delays at Spaghetti Junction, by using the M5.

The opening of the M6(Toll) to the north should help reduce this problem

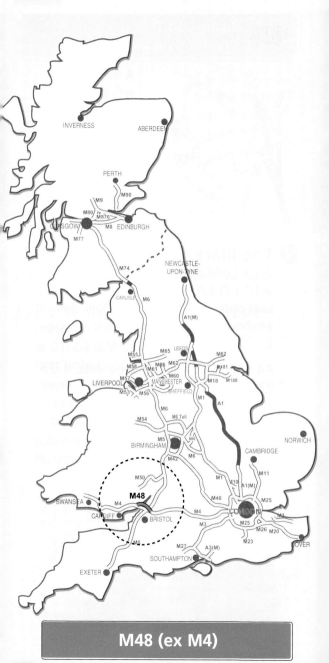

M48 (ex M4)

Aust to Chepstow

1   Avonmouth A403

This used to be the last junction on the M4 before crossing over into Wales. With the building of another bridge over the Severn, this section was renamed M48 and the new section became the M4.

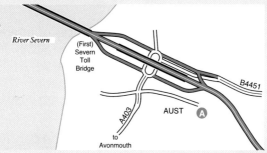

Places of interest
St Augustine's Vineyard 1m

Boars Head
Aust
☎ 01454 632 278
Last orders: 2.15pm and 9.15pm.
No evening meals on Sundays.
£££

A late 18th Century pub which probably was a coaching stop for those crossing over to Wales on the ferry. It gives a friendly welcome to all, enhanced in winter by log fires and home made cooking.

There is outside seating where dogs are welcome.

2   Chepstow A48

Chepstow, just off the junction, is well worth a visit especially the castle. There are other restaurants, hotels and pubs in the town.

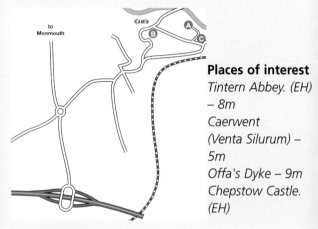

Places of interest
Tintern Abbey. (EH) – 8m
Caerwent (Venta Silurum) – 5m
Offa's Dyke – 9m
Chepstow Castle. (EH)

Ⓐ Wye Knot
Chepstow
☎ 01291 622 929
Last orders: 2.00pm and 10.00pm. Closed Sunday evening and all day Monday.
£££

A privately owned restaurant on the banks of the River Wye with a varied menu cooked by two award winning chefs. A plaque on the wall outside says that the Chartists sailed from here in 1840 for Tasmania.
Well-behaved children welcome but dogs outside.
Booking advisable.

2 Chepstow A48

B Castle View Hotel
Chepstow
☎ 01291 620 349
Last orders: 2.00pm and 9.30pm.
Residents only for Sunday evenings.
£££

As the name implies, it really does have a view up to the castle. Some 350 years old, it has been modernised to provide 13 bedrooms mostly in annexes. Outside there is a beer garden at the rear, whilst indoors there is a restaurant and a bar. There are facilities for the disabled. Children and dogs are welcome.

C Boat Inn
Chepstow
☎ 01291 628 192
Last orders: 3.00pm and 9.30pm.
9.00pm on Sundays.
£££

A Free House which was built in 1789 so it has flagged stone floors and an old fashioned Snug with an open fire. Upstairs in a modern part is a restaurant which specialises in fish. It overlooks the river and has outside seating. Children but no dogs.

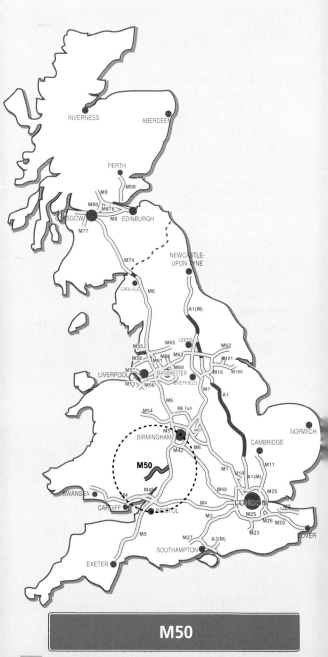

M50

M5 to Ross on Wye

Junctions 1 to 4

The M50 was one of the first motorways to be built and for some years was in splendid isolation until joined to the M 5. It was built to connect the Midlands with South Wales but only goes as far as Ross on Wye before continuing as dual-carriageway to Newport. It is also a way of driving to Wales without paying the toll charges levied on the Severn Bridges!

There are a plenty of places to see, not too far from the motorway. Ross on Wye is a market town with interesting old buildings. Nearby is picturesque Symons Yat where the river Wye winds through a gorge below the imposing ruins of Goodrich Castle.
To the south is the Forest of Dean famous amongst other things for the small family coal mines still in private ownership.
To the west is the town of Monmouth with its medieval bridge and further on the ruins of Raglan Castle destroyed by Cromwell.

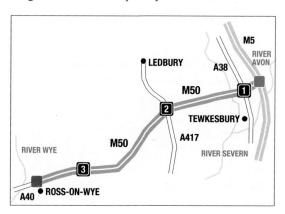

1   Malvern   Tewkesbury A38

A relatively easy junction. Just follow the signs to
Twyning. The Fleet Inn is brown signed from the
roundabout.

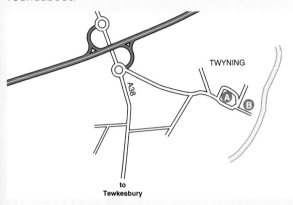

Places of interest
Tewkesbury Abbey – 3m

Ⓐ **The Village Inn**
Twyning
☎ 01684 293 500
Last orders: 2.30pm and 10.00pm.
Closed Mondays and Tuesdays for lunch.
£

Overlooking the village green, it was
once a bakery, then a shop and
Post office and is now a
friendly old
fashioned pub.
Best to check
on their
opening
hours.

1 Malvern   Tewkesbury A38

B The Fleet Inn
Twyning
☎ 01684 274 310
Last orders: 9.00pm. in the restaurant.
££ 🦴

By the side of the River Avon, it is a
popular place, with some bedrooms. An
open area for bar meals and outside
seating on a terrace by the banks of the
river. Dogs allowed on leads.

Hereford A438 Ledbury A417
Gloucester A417

Take the road to Gloucester to find the Rose and
Crown which is about a mile from the junction

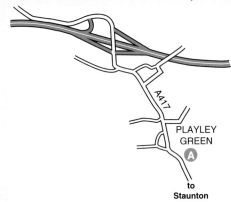

Places of interest
Eastnor Castle. (HHA) – 5m

 The Rose and Crown
Redmarly D'Abitot
☎ 01531 650 234
Last orders: 2.00pm and9.15pm
No evening meals on Sundays.
££

A simple wayside pub dating from the 1800s
with the addition of a later Assembly Room
which is now the restaurant. Now owned by
Pubmasters, it has a bar and outside
seating. Dogs
and children
allowed. It has
recently
changed
management.

3 Newent B4221

The only T junction exit in the U.K which is known in the trade as a Compact Grade Separation! Take the road to Kilcot.

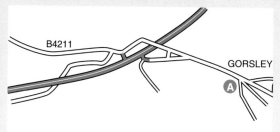

B4211

GORSLEY

A

A

The Roadmaker Inn

Gorsley

☎ 01989 720 352

Last orders: 2.00pm and 9.00pm

No food on Monday nights.

££

The Roadmaker was built in 1840 by a roadbuilder hence the name. Now it is a family run public house and offers a warm welcome with fresh home cooked food and bar snacks.

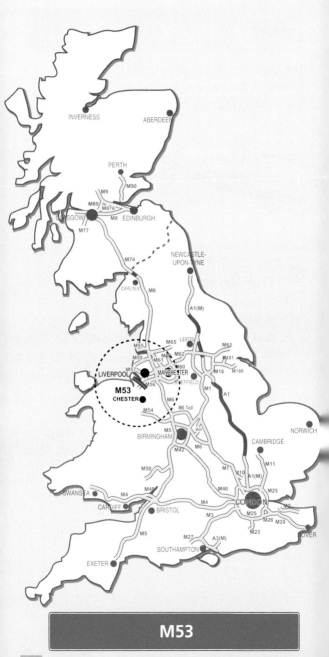

M53

Birkenhead to Chester

Junctions 1 to 12

This short 12 mile stretch of motorway is interesting as it passes through the densely industrialised area of Ellesmere Port as well as some pleasant wooded countryside. Port Sunlight is the home of soap and the Leverhulmes' amazing house and art collection. There are apparently more millionaires in the Wirral than elsewhere in the UK excluding the London area.

At the other end of the motorway is Chester, still a walled city with medieval buildings and once the home base of the Roman XX (Victrix) Legion.

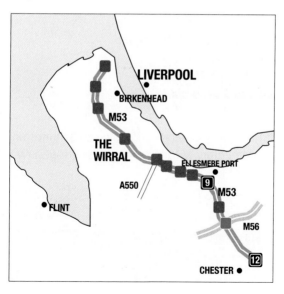

| 9 | **Ellesmere Port**
Boat Museum A5032 |

Just follow the signs to the Boat Museum, which is well worth a visit.

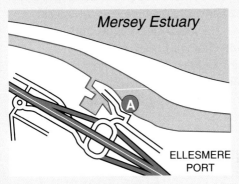

Mersey Estuary

ELLESMERE PORT

Places of interest
The Boat Museum.

Ⓐ **Rotate Restaurant**
Ellesmere Port
☎ 01513 551 163
Last orders: 9.30pm.
£

It has changed hands and now concentrates on contemporary Mediterranean cuisine especially for light lunches.

Birkenhead to Chester

12 Chester A56

There is a danger of continuing past the junction onto the dual carriageway A55 to Wales.

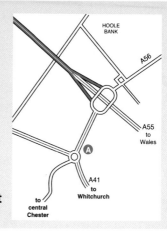

HOOLE BANK

A56

A55 to Wales

A41 to Whitchurch

to central Chester

Places of interest
Chester – 1m

Ⓐ Hoole Hall Hotel

Chester
☎ 01244 408 800
Last orders: 2.00pm and 9.15pm.
£££

In 1785, it was the home of the pioneer balloonist the Reverend Thomas Baldwin. In the last war it was occupied by the Army and remained derelict for many years. It was rebuilt in 1990 as a hotel set in five acres of garden, with 97 bedrooms and a conference centre. Bar meals can be made available in the lounge bar.

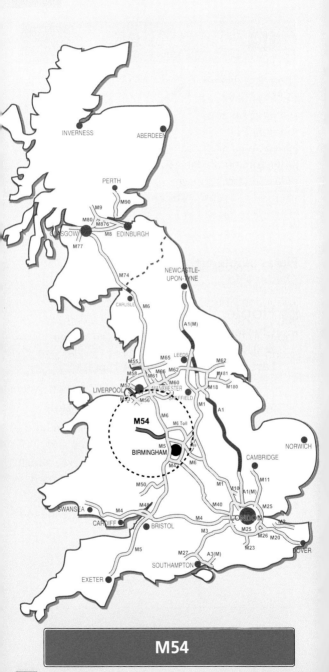

M54

Wolverhampton to Telford

Junctions 1 to 7

A 23 mile stretch of motorway which was opened in 1975 to link Birmingham to Shrewsbury and Wales. Beyond Telford it has been upgraded to a modern dual carriageway to the other side of Shrewsbury.

After coming off the M6 it passes through pleasant farming countryside until the much vaunted Telford New Town, which is typical of 1960s planning - interminable tree lined roads and roundabouts with sparse signing.

The countryside around is well worth a visit. Bridgnorth, reduced by Cromwell; the Ironbridge Gorge, the cradle of modern industry and medieval Much Wenlock with its Priory. To the west of Telford rises the Wrekin, acting as the gateway to the Welsh Border and close by, the ruins of the Roman administrative town of Wroxeter with its massive public baths. Shrewsbury itself is one of the most attractive county towns in England with a wealth of old buildings.

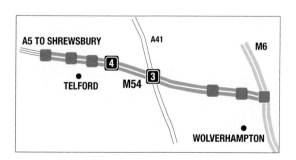

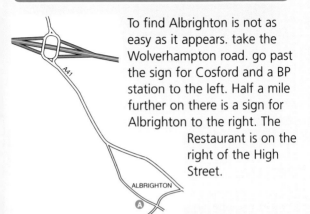

To find Albrighton is not as easy as it appears. take the Wolverhampton road. go past the sign for Cosford and a BP station to the left. Half a mile further on there is a sign for Albrighton to the right. The Restaurant is on the right of the High Street.

Places of interest *Weston Park. (HHA) – 3m Boscobel House and the Royal Oak Tree – 4m Aerospace Museum. Lillieshall Abbey – ½m*

 Frederiques
Albrighton
☎ 01902 375 522
Last orders: 2.00pm and 10.00pm. 3.00pm on Sunday but closed in the evening
£££

A deservedly popular restaurant in the centre of this once rural village. Modern decor and chairs but comfortable and attractive. Children but no dogs.

4 Telford East A464
Kidderminster A442 Ironbridge

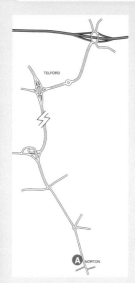

Get off the M54 at Junction 4 and take the A442 to Bridgnorth, winding around several roundabouts and with endless avenues leading off in different directions. Norton is about 8 miles south

Places of interest

*Bridgnorth,
Iron Bridge.*

Ⓐ Hundred House Hotel
Norton
☎ 01952 730 353
Last orders: 2.15pm and 9.15pm every day.
£££

Dating back to the 14 century, it was once a courthouse and the stocks are still in place on the other side of the road. It is now a friendly family hotel with 10 bedrooms, two dining areas and a bar.
Children allowed and
dogs at a charge.
Parking for
horseboxes
and
caravans.

M56

Manchester to Chester

Some 37 miles long, it connects Manchester with the commuter areas of Cheshire as well as Chester and North Wales beyond. It is not particularly attractive especially when coming out of Manchester past the Airport. However once over the intersection with the M6 (a complicated junction, badly signed) it gets slightly better. At the end of the motorway it continues into Wales as a dual carriageway.

The historic city of Chester was once the base of the Roman XX (Victrix) Legion. It still has its medieval walls and was where the architect Sir John Vanbrugh grew up.

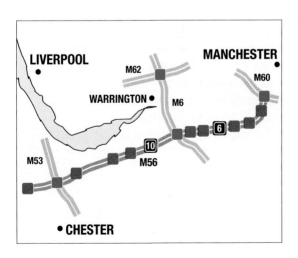

6 Wilmslow Macclesfield
Hale A538

A certain amount of skill is required to negotiate
the roundabouts and you may miss the turn off
down Sunbank Lane.

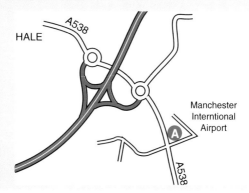

Ⓐ The Romper
Hale Barns
☎ 01619 806 806
Last orders: 11,00pm. 10.30pm on Sundays.
ff

Owned now by Scottish and Newcastle, it was
once an old fashioned pub in a backwater but
has been enlarged and well modernised,
complete with dried hops. There is a beer
garden and a large car park.
Dogs are welcome outside as well as children.

Manchester to Chester

10 Northwich   Warrington A49

The Birch and Bottle seems to be further than one expects, but keep on. There are some new purpose built Road Houses as well, visible from the junction.

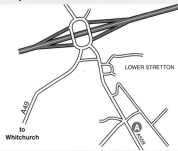

Places of interest
Anderton Boat Lift (EH) – 5m;
Arley Hall. (HHA) – 7m

Ⓐ Birch and Bottle
Lower Stretton
☎ 01925 730 225
Last orders: 3.00pm and 11.00pm.
10.30 on Sundays.
££

Owned by Greenalls, it is a cheerful place with a restaurant in the conservatory, where you can enjoy their speciality (Black Pudding). This place could date from 1814 as a wayside pub. There is outside seating for the hardy and his dog.

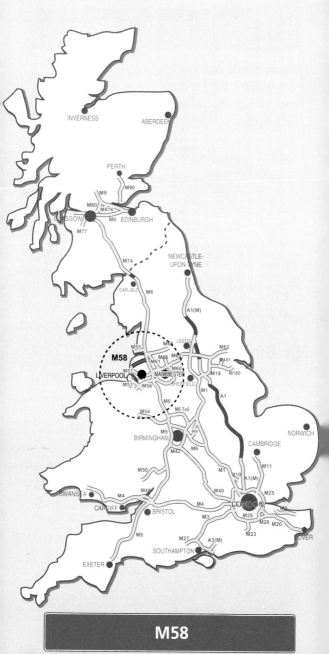

M58

Liverpool to Wigan

Junctions 1 to 5

Not the most exciting motorway, but it fulfills a useful function of linking Liverpool with the M6 by Wigan. It starts near the Aintree Racecourse, the venue for the Grand National, where it intersects with the M57, which is the western section of a non existent ring road around Liverpool.

It would be nice to be able to rattle off a list of places to visit off the motorway to reduce the tedium but that is not possible. The best hope is to look forward to lunch or dinner or else to drive into Wigan, long the butt of Music Hall humour but curiously enough not nearly so bad as its reputation.

Liverpool itself must be worth a visit if only to see the Tate of the North in its new home in the Docks, which is a magnificent example of what can be done with imagination and foresight.

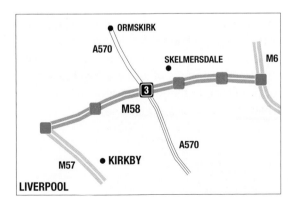

3 St. Helens   Ormskirk A570
Southport

You might miss the Quattro Restaurant, which is on what looks like a layby to the left as soon as you get off the roundabout.

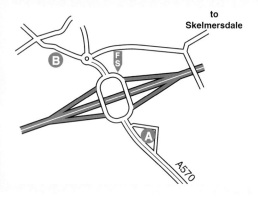

Quattro
Bickerstaffe
☎ 01695 720 800
Last orders: 2.00pm and 10.30pm.
Closed Mondays and Saturdays for lunch.
£££

As the name implies, it is an Italian restaurant with the usual cheerful atmosphere. It relies on its food, rather than beer gardens and the like, to attract customers of which some fifty can lunch or dine at the same time.
Children and dogs are welcome.

---

3 St. Helens   Ormskirk A570
Southport

B **The Sandpiper**
Bickerstaffe
☎ 01695 733 666
Last orders: 10.00pm. 9.30pm on
Sundays.
££

Once a farmhouse, it is now one of the
modern generation of purpose designed
pubs with outside seating in a garden and
a large carpark.
It has a friendly atmosphere and
welcomes dogs outdoors. Bar meals
served all day in an open plan bar area
where you can still smoke.

Parts of the ringroad had been known in the past as the M63 and the M62, as well as the M66. It has now been renumbered after the completion of the entire Orbital Motorway as the M60 and the old junction numbers have also been changed. Even the section of the M62, which bypassed Manchester to the north, is numbered M60. The M67 to the east had nothing that we could find. Even the M66 with such names as Ramsbottom was a disappointment. It would be best to hurry round Manchester, as the only place which gives any hint of a comfort stop would be Jacksons Boat at Sale.

6 (ex 8) Sale A144

The access to Jacksons Boat is down a narrow country lane past a golf course to the right.

Ⓐ Jacksons Boat
Sale
☎ 0161 973 8549
Last call: 11.00pm
£

This simple pub must once have been frequented by bargees plying their trade on the River Mersey. For the time being no food is being served. There is a playground and a large beer garden where both dogs and children can stretch their legs.

233

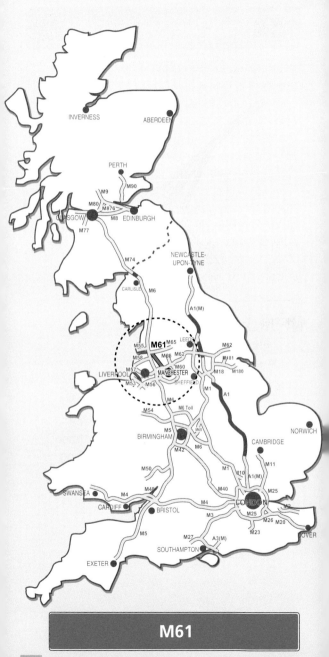

M61

Manchester to Preston

Junctions 1 to 9

A useful motorway for those living in and around Manchester who are going to or coming from the Lake District or the north. It is also an alternative for motorists driving over the Pennines on the M62 to connect with the M1 or the M6. Apart from that there is little that can be said for it.

About the only redeeming feature is the sight of the Pennines to the east looming over the outer suburbs of Manchester and Bolton. The place names such as Whittle-le-Woods or Bottom o' th' Moor have a certain charm.

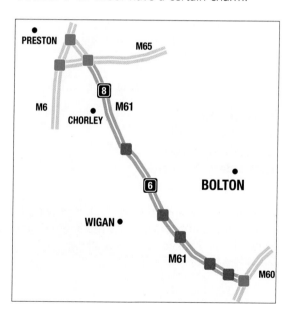

6   Chorley   Horwich A6027
Bolton North

An uninteresting junction, but the view across to
the Pennines over the Reebok Football Stadium is
good.

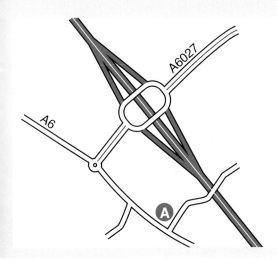

A Royal Oak
West Houghton
☎ 01942 812 168
Last orders: 10.00pm.
££

A wayside stop since the 1830s, it is now part
of a Group and has been fully modernised and
serves home cooked bar meals all day.

> **8** Leyland Southport A6
> Chorley A6

The Red Cat requires concentration as you have to drive past it and then come round behind it.

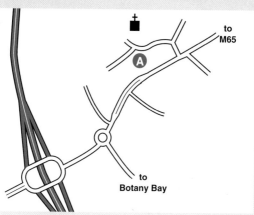

Ⓐ **Red Cat** ⋆
Witterly Woods
☎ 01257 263 966
Last orders: 2.00pm and 10.00pm.
11.00pm on Sundays.
ff

There has been an inn here since 1805 and is now a cheerful Italian place obviously specialising in Italian food served in the flagstoned eating areas. There is a playground and outside seating where dogs are encouraged.

M62

Liverpool to Hull

One of the few motorways which run laterally across the country. It is 108 miles long and was completed in 1976 to link the ports of Liverpool and Hull. It does not lend itself to gastronomic feasts.

WESTERN SECTION   1 to 26

With the best will in the world this part, from Liverpool to beyond Manchester, is not pretty. However once past Junction 21 it climbs up into the Pennines and Junction 22 could be a remote spot for picnics near the top, but marred by endless road lights on the motorway. It then descends into the industrial area of Huddersfield and Bradford.

9 Warrington A49
Newton

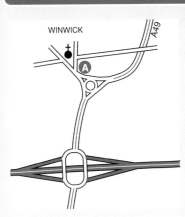

Head for the Church. The Swan is on the road forking to the right.

Ⓐ The Swan
Winwick
☎ 01925 631 416
Last orders: 10.00pm. 9.30pm on Sundays.
££ 🛏

The present building dates from 1898 and is owned by the Chef and Brewer chain. There are 42 double bedrooms in a modern extension, with a restaurant and a bar in the older part. It also caters for conferences. Some outside seating where dogs are permitted.

Liverpool to Hull

> **21** Milnrow
> Shaw A640

Not as difficult as it looks, but the road through this ex mining town needs concentration.

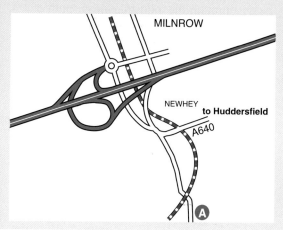

Ⓐ The Jubilee
Shaw
☎ 01706 847 540
Last orders: 2.00pm. No meals on Saturdays.
££

So named after the Jubilee Colliery which is down the road but now closed. It is open for lunches only and closed on Saturdays. Privately owned it gives a friendly welcome to visitors. It specialises in leg of lamb served in the restaurant cum bar. Outside seating where dogs are welcome.

EASTERN SECTION 27 to 38

Not the most attractive part of England as it passes through the industrial areas south of Leeds. However once past the intersection with the A1(M) and the famous Ferrybridge Power Station, the surroundings become more rural, excepting the odd slag heap or power station. It is flat and level full of drainage ditches and fens.

The M62 crosses over the Humber at Goole with views over the surrounding countryside. The tower of the Minster at Howden is impressive and the inland port of Goole is to the south made visible by the cranes.

The motorway ceases just short of Brough, an old Roman town which was the ferry point for those crossing over the Humber in those days. It continues as a dual carriageway to Hull and the ferry port for Rotterdam.

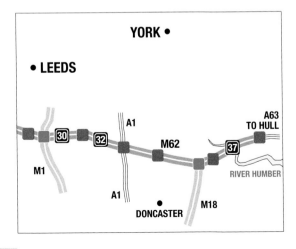

30 Rothwell
    Wakefield A642

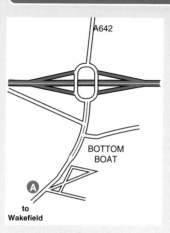

A642

BOTTOM
BOAT

A

to
Wakefield

Easy enough to
find the Spindle
Tree.

 Spindle Tree
Stanley
☎ 01924 824 810
Last orders: 2.00pm and 9.00pm
Sundays 8.00pm
ff

A small wayside pub now owned by
Punch Taverns. They have refurbished it
with open areas for eating and a bar. It
has a cheerful and friendly atmosphere.
Outside seating in a garden at the rear.

32   Pontefract   Castleford A639

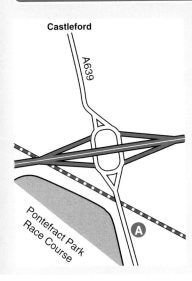

Castleford

A639

Pontefract Park
Race Course

Ⓐ

Handy for those
going to the
Races.

Places of interest
*Pontefract
Racecourse – 1m*

Ⓐ Parkside Hotel
Pontefract
☎ 01977 709 911
Last orders: 2.30pm and 9.00pm.
ff 🛏

A privately owned modernised hotel with 29
bedrooms, a restaurant and a Long Bar where
bar meals are served. A playground, beer
garden, outside seating and a large car park
are overlooked by what was one of the last
remaining working coal mines. Children
welcome.

37 Howden A614 Selby A63 York A63 Bridlington

Howden was once famous for one of Europe's largest horse fairs until some twenty years ago when it had degenerated into a one-horse town. It is now a thriving picturesque place.

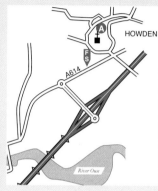

Places of interest
*Howden Minster.
The former
Summer Palace
of the Bishops of
Durham.*

 ## Sweet Thoughts
Howden
☎ 01430 431 615
Last orders: 9.00am to 4.00pm. Closed Mondays and Tuesdays.
£

A small Tea Room in the centre of Howden which serves breakfasts, morning coffee, light lunches and afternoon tea. It is all home baked on the premises by the owner, which makes a refreshing change.
Children but no dogs.

M65

Preston to Colne

Junctions 1 to 14

For many years the M65 was a short isolated stretch from Blackburn to Colne. t has now been continued to link with the M6 at Preston.

There is not much to say about it except that you are driving through the last remaining vestiges of the Lancashire cotton industry with huge palatial factories of Italianate architecture. The comforting sight of the Pennines which is visible on both sides of the motorway is welcoming.

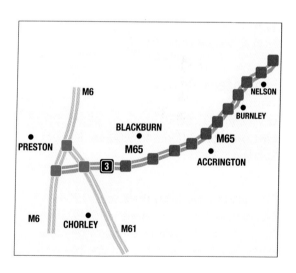

3   Blackburn   Bolton A675

The roundabout at the end of the lead off could be confusing.

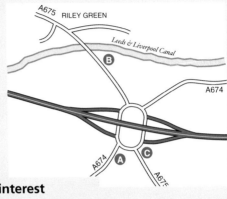

Places of interest
Hoghton Tower. (HHA) – 2m

Ⓐ Hoghton Arms
Withnell
☎ 01254 201 083
Last orders: 12.00pm to 9.00pm. 8.00pm on Sundays.
££

The building has been there since 1704 and has been a pub long before 1910. Recently it has been greatly extended to provide more eating areas with a restaurant and bar with fires but of the gas log variety. Outside seating and a garden.
Parking for
caravans
and
horseboxes.

3 Blackburn Bolton A675

Ⓑ The Boatyard Inn
Riley Green
☎ 01254 209 841
Last orders: 9.30pm. 9pm on Fridays.
££

Once a boat yard by the Leeds and Liverpool
Canal, it has now part of a group and has
been converted into a waterside inn with
large open areas. Dogs allowed outdoors
but children not
encouraged,
for obvious
reasons.

Ⓒ Ristorante Alghergo
Withnell
☎ 01254 202 222
Last orders: 10.30pm (Dinners only)
On Sundays from 12.00am to 10.00pm.
£££

As the name implies this is an Italian
restaurant which has a good local
reputation and a friendly atmosphere.

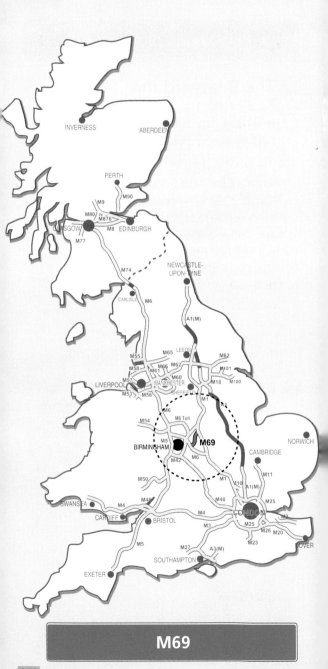

M69

Coventry to Leicester

Junctions 1 to 2

This motorway was built in the mid 1970s to give direct access between Coventry and Leicester. It is comparatively little used so is useful to those who are on the M1 or M40 as a means of driving north or south.

The junction with the M1 is rather abrupt as a result of a decision at the time not to make it into a proper clover leaf as the volume of traffic would not warrant the expense.

The building of the motorways has had the curious effect of isolating corners of the countryside to create rural areas of calm, such as the part around Bosworth Field ("-my Kingdom for a horse").

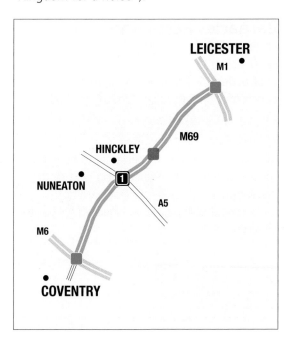

1   Nuneaton   Hinckley

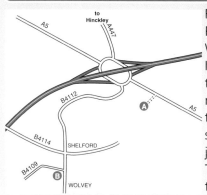

For the Blue Pig take the Wolvey road. In the village there is a modern pub to the right and a sharp turning just beyond it. Turn right and the Blue Pig is down the road to the left.

Places of interest *Bosworth Field 1485 – 8m*

Ⓐ Barnacles Restaurant
Nr Hinckley
☎ 01455 633 220
Last orders: 2.00pm and 9.00pm.
Lunch only on Saturdays. Closed Sundays.
£££

A privately owned restaurant in pleasant grounds with a lake. It specialises in fish and there is a separately owned shop next to the restaurant which sells fish. Dogs are not welcomed and there are no special facilities for children.

1   Nuneaton   Hinckley

B **The Blue Pig**
Wolvey
☎ 01455 220 256
Last orders: 2.00pm and 8.30pm on
Mondays and Tuesdays. 9.00pm on
Wednesday to Friday. 9.30pm on Saturday
and closed on Sunday night.
££

An old coaching inn dating from the 15th
century. It has a restaurant and a bar
serving home cooked specials and Real
Ales. It is family run so is friendly and the
original beams give it an even better
atmosphere. Outside seating and a garden
at the back. Dogs allowed and children
for meals.

M180

M18 to Grimsby

A short 27 mile stretch from the M18 towards Grimsby, the last 15 miles being dual carriageway. It begins at the intersection with the M18, then crosses flat fenlands which were drained by the Dutch, before passing the much maligned steelworks town of Scunthorpe. It goes through pleasant wooded expanses of countryside to Junction 5. From there it continues as a dual carriageway to Grimsby and the link road to the Humber Bridge and Hull leads off to the left. (The Whistle and Flute in Barnetby le Wold will give you lunch and dinner.)

There are some interesting places to see in the neighbourhood, such as the Saxon church at Barton on Humber, the imposing intact brick gatehouse of Thornton Abbey and the old market town of Brigg.

Those with a knowledge of Roman history will know that at Junction 4 the motorway crosses over Ermine Street from Lincoln to the crossing point over the Humber to Brough.

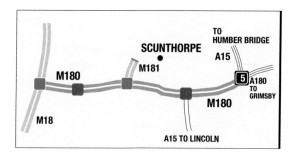

5 Humber Bridge   Hull A15
Grimsby A180

Easy enough to find the Railway Inn which is
down the village street to the left. The Whistle
& Flute is opposite the station.

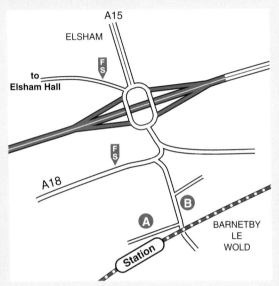

Places of interest
Elsham Hall (HHA)

5 Humber Bridge   Hull A15
Grimsby A180

Ⓐ The Railway Inn
Barnetby-le-Wold
☎ 01652 688 284
Last orders: No lunches on weekdays.
Otherwise 9.00pm. On Saturdays 2.00pm
and 9.00pm. No evening meals on
Sundays and Tuesdays.
£

A tenanted pub of Enterprise Inns. Food
served in the dining areas, which
have interesting memorabilia.
A large car park adjacent
which can take
horse boxes.

Ⓑ Whistle & Flute
Barnetby-le-Wold
☎ 01652 688 238
Last orders: 2.00pm and 9.30pm. 2.30pm
and 9.00pm on Sundays.
£

As the name implies it is by the station
which still functions, but not too noisily. It
is a family owned hotel which has 14
double bedrooms. There is a restaurant
and a bar where home cooked food and
fresh vegetables are served. Outside there
is a playground and seating
where children and
dogs may roam.

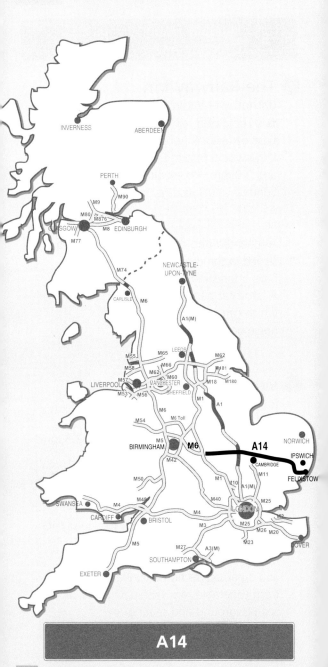

A14

Midlands to Felixtowe

This is a dual carriageway, as opposed to a motorway, but the junctions have now been numbered. It has become the main link between the Midlands and the port of Felixtowe.

This section between the M1 and A1 passes through the old hunting country of the shires such as the Pytchley Hunt, which could soon be abolished.

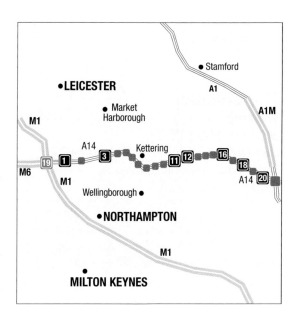

M1/19 Felixtowe   Corby
Kettering   A14

A transitional junction which is shortly to be
reconstructed to make it easier for those using
the M1 or the M6 to access the A14.

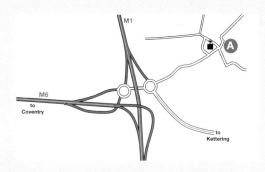

Places of interest
Stamford Hall

The Chequers
Swinford
☎ 01788 860 318
Last Orders: 2.00pm and 9.00pm,
No evening meals on Sundays.
Closed Monday lunch
£

Traditionally friendly village pub with pub
games. gas log fires and Real Ale, serving
meals in the bar or in the dining area. Garden
and a playground where dogs
and children are welcome.

1 Welford 5199

Just drive south to Thornby and the Red Lion is to the left.

Places of interest

Naseby Battlefind.1645 – 1 mile
Cottesbrooke Hall (HA) – 3 miles
Holdenby House (HHA) – 5 miles

B The Red Lion
Thornby
☎ 01604 740 238
Last orders: 2.30pm and 9.30pm.
No evening meals on Sundays. Closed Mondays.
££

A traditional village pub which is family managed. It has a restaurant and a bar where bar meals can be had. There is a beer garden at the back. No dogs. The owner has an interest in Rugby and classic cars. The car park will take horseboxes.

3 **Leicester   Mkt Harb'oro**
Desborough   A6

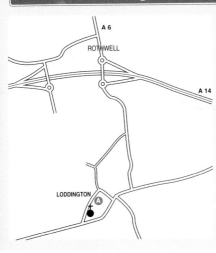

Head for the spire of the church and the inn is to the north of it.

Ⓐ The Hare
Loddington
☎ 01536 710 337
Last orders: 2.30pm and 10.00pm.
£££

A privately owned inn which has a good reputation for good food and specialises in fish and game. For those in a hurry there are bar meals and sandwiches. Outside seating and a garden. Dogs allowed. A large car park for caravans and horseboxes.

11 Wellingb'oro A510

A motorway type junction so no difficulties.

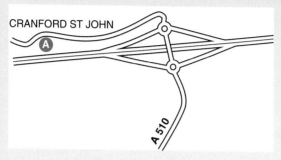

Places of interest
Boughton House (HA) – 4 miles

Ⓐ Red Lion

Cranford St John
☎ 01536 330 663
Last orders: 2.00pm and 9.00pm.
No evening meals on Sundays. Closed
Mondays.
££

An old 16th century pub, now part of
Punch. A friendly welcome in the beamed
restaurant area and bar. They specialise in
fish. Outside seating and a
large car park. No dogs
allowed but a
childrens' play
area in
the garden.

12 Great Corby A6116

No problems with the junctions as it is similar to motorways. Turn right at the roundabout.

Places of interest
Lyveden new Bield (NT) – 7 miles

Ⓐ The Woolpack
Islip
☎ 01832 732 578
Last orders: 2.30pm and 9.30pm. 10.00pm on Fridays and Saturdays. 9.00pm on Sundays.
£££ 🛏

A family run pub with a restaurant on the first floor and two bars below with beams and flag stoned floors serving bar meals. It has 8 bedrooms, a beer garden, outside seating and a car park for horseboxes and caravans. Well behaved children indoors and dogs outside.

16 Kimbolton   Old Weston B660

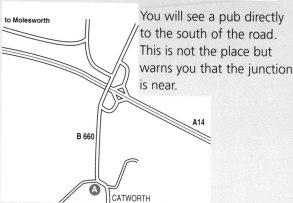

to Molesworth

You will see a pub directly to the south of the road. This is not the place but warns you that the junction is near.

A14

B 660

Ⓐ CATWORTH

Places of interest

Kimbolton Castle – 4 miles

Ⓐ **The Racehorse Country Inn**
Catworth

☎ 01832 710 123

Last orders: 2.00pm and 9.00pm. 2.30pm on Sundays but no evening meals. Closed for food on Mondays.

£££ 🛏

A family run traditional village pub with 5 bedrooms. Cheerful atmosphere and a warm welcome. Outside seating and a car park at rear. Children welcome but dogs outside.

17 Leighton Bromswold

Getting off and on when driving eastwards is easy but more complicated from the east.

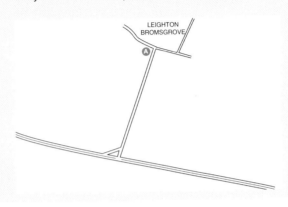

Ⓐ The Green Man

Leighton Bromswold
☎ 01480 890 238
Last orders: 2.00pm for lunch, only on Fridays, Saturdays and Sundays. 9.00pm. No evening meal on Sundays. Closed Mondays.
£

Built in 1605 it has low beams, log fires, old fashioned pub memorabilia and a friendly welcome from the family. A childrens room inside and outside seating with a garden.

18 Spaldwick Magna Stow

Drive to the village and the Geroge Inn is on the left opposite the village green

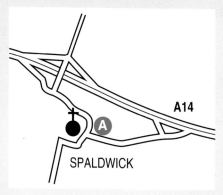

A14

SPALDWICK

Ⓐ The George Inn
Spaldwick
☎ 01480 890 293
Last orders: 2.30pm and 10.00pm.
9.00pm on Sundays.
£££

This 16th century inn is now part of the Spirit Group and has been extensively refurbished. However there is still an atmosphere of log fires and beams. Outside seating. Dogs and children allowed and the car park will take horseboxes.

20 Ellington

No difficulty. Just head for the church.

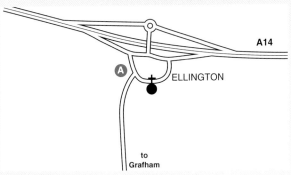

Places of interest
Grafham Water

The Mermaid
Ellington
☎ 01480 891 450
Last orders: 2.00pm and 9.30pm daily
£££ 🍴

A traditional family run old English pub
specialising in fish. Built in the 13c it has low
beams, log fires in winter and serves Real Ales.
Outside seating and a garden. On street
parking.

Midlands to Felixtowe

This part goes past Huntingdon, Cambridge and Newmarket to Bury St Edmunds. It is a busy section especially when it joins the M11.

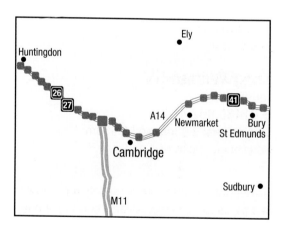

26&27 Fenstanton Fen Drayton
Swavesey Boxworth Elsworth

You can get to the King William IV by using either junction.

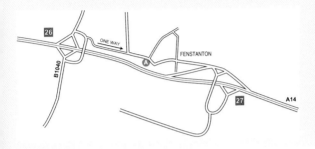

Ⓐ King William IV
Fenstanton
☎ 01480 462 467
Last orders: 2.15pm and 9.45pm.
No evening meals on Sundays.
£££

A cheerful 17c pub with a friendly atmosphere in a picturesque village. Beams and inglenook fires. They specialise in home made puddings and sandwiches. Children and dogs allowed.

41 Saxham   Risby

Should be fairly simpe as it is on the way into
the village.

Places of interest
Ickworth (NT) – 4 miles

 # Crown & Castle
Risby
☎ 01284 810 393
Last orders: 2.00pm and 9.00pm. No
evening meals on Sundays.
££

A managed house of Greene King which
changed hands some two years ago. Since
then there have been improvements and it
has a good local reputation. Outside
seating in the front, a garden and the car
park is at the rear. Children welcomed.

Western Section   43   60

From Bury St Edmunds to Felixtowe it passes
through a rural area of Suffolk. It goes past
Ipswich to the north before crossing over the
River Orwell.

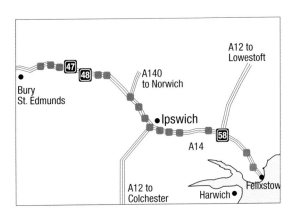

47 Ixworth A1088

Take the A1088 to Norton and The Dog is to your right as you come into the village.

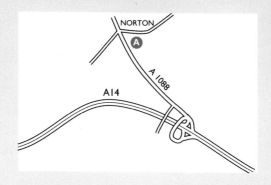

Ⓐ The Dog
Norton
☎ 01349 230 440
Last orders: 2.00pm and 9.00pm daily
££

A tenanted 16th century pub of Greene King serving home cooked meals in the dining areas of bare brick walls and low beams. A garden and large car park so suitable for horseboxes. Children allowed.

48   Haughley   Bacton

You will have to cross over the central carriageway if coming from Felixtowe. Bear right at the entrance to the village and the Restaurant is to your left opposite the village green.

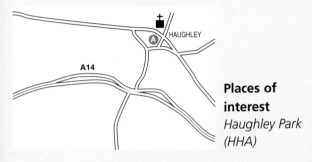

Places of interest
Haughley Park (HHA)

Ⓐ The Old Counting House Restaurant

Haughley
☎ 01449 673 617
Last orders: 2.30pm and 10.00pm daily.
Closed on Tuesday.
£££

A family run no-smoking restaurant in a 700 year house which was a medieval Bank, hence the name. It was then a shop before becoming a restaurant which it has been for the past hundred years. It has an imaginative menu which children may also enjoy. A garden at the back but on street parking.

58 Lowestoft   Woodbridge A12

The Ship is signposted from the main road. At Levington bear left and pass the church.

Places of interest
Levington Lagoon

Ⓐ The Ship *
Levington
☎ 01473 659 573
Last orders: 2.00pm and 9.30pm.
No evening meals on Sundays
££

An old inn with a smugglers room upstairs. Fresh home cooked meals specialising in fish, served in the dining areas featuring nautical memorabilia. In the last hundred years it has only changed hands four times. Outside seating and a garden where children and dogs must remain.

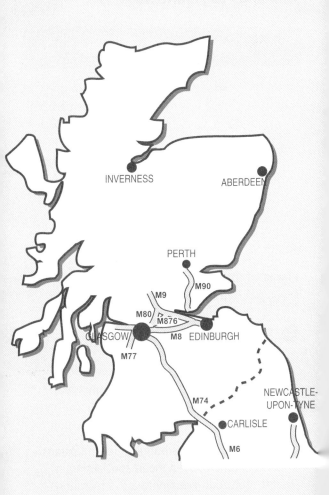

THE MOTORWAY NETWORK

Scotland

Motorway introduction

Scotland may extend a warm welcome to visitors and even Sassenachs, but for the motorway user you get the impression that the Scots have forgotten the art of hospitality to the passing traveller. Part of this impression may be due to the fact that the new motorways, except for the M74, do not follow the old coaching routes. There are some excellent exceptions to the rule but there were a lot of places which did not come up to scratch. On the M8 for example, from Edinburgh to Glasgow, there is not one single place worthy of being mentioned.

The most tedious aspect of the Scottish motorways is the system of linked junctions. It might save money but it generates unnecessary driving on minor roads.

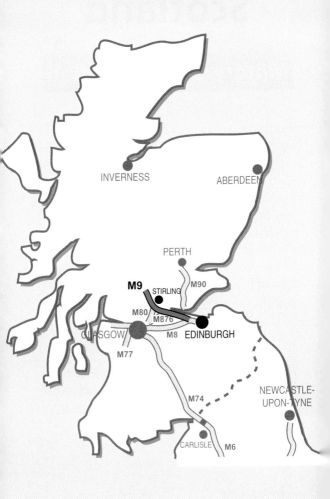

M9

Edinburgh to Stirling

Junctions 1 to 11

Starting near the Airport it passes through agricultural country and old shale heaps.

You then drive past the impressive ruins of Linlithgow Palace, once one of the great buildings of Europe, admired by the French princesses who were married to Scottish kings. It was burnt in 1745 during the Jacobite Rebellion and has been roofless ever since, but there are rumours that parts could be re-roofed.

The motorway ends north of the equally impressive Stirling Castle, the favourite refuge for the Scottish kings, which was remodelled by James V and is a fine example of Renaissance architecture.

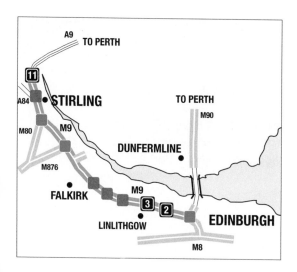

2. Forth Rd Bridge (A904)
3. Linlithgow A803   Bo'ness

Like most of the junctions these are linked together, depending upon the direction of travel. Apart from the one mentioned below, there are other places in Linlithgow to suit most requirements.

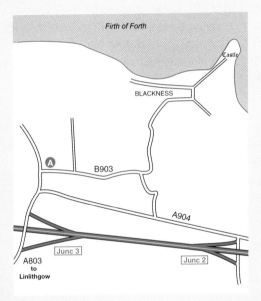

Places of interest
Hopetoun House (HHA) – 4m
The House of The Binns (NTS) – 1m
Blackness Castle(HS) – 2m
Linlithgow Palace(HS) – 2m

2. Forth Rd Bridge (A904)
3. Linlithgow A803   Bo'ness

Champany Inn *

Champany
☎ 01506 834 532
Last orders: 2.00pm and 10.00pm.
The main restaurant is not open on
Sundays
nor Saturday Lunch.
££££

It is one of the best known restaurants in
Scotland. It was once a farm house where
Mary Queen of Scots used to come over
from Linlithgow to have picnics, hence the
name. The Inn also has 16 bedrooms
should you not be tempted to drive on
again after dinner. There is outside seating
for hot days as well as a Bistro to suit the
more hurried motorist. It is noted for
Aberdeen Angus beef and has been
named as Meat Restaurant of Great
Britain as well as Best Restaurant of the
Year.

11 Doune B824 Dunblane B8033 Bridge of Allan A9

After coming off the roundabout, drive towards the outskirts of the Bridge of Allan. Just before the said bridge, with a high wooded bluff on the other side of the river, turn right. The Inn is to the right.

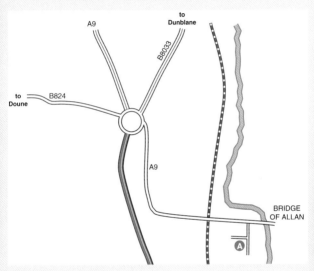

Places of interest

Doune Castle - 3m
Stirling Castle (HS) – 2m
Argyll's Lodging (HS) – 2m
The Wallace Monument – 2m

Doune B824 Dunblane B8033 Bridge of Allan A9

Ⓐ **The Old Bridge Inn**
Bridge of Allan
☎ 01786 833 335
Last orders: 2.30pm and 8.45pm.
£££

The Inn was built in 1710 by the bridge which was first constructed in 1520 and rebuilt in 1695. It was originally surrounded by mills and by Willie's brewery, famous for making good beer. The interior has been stripped out to make a larger area with rough stone walls and timber panelling to form a comfortable restaurant/bar. It has recently changed hands.

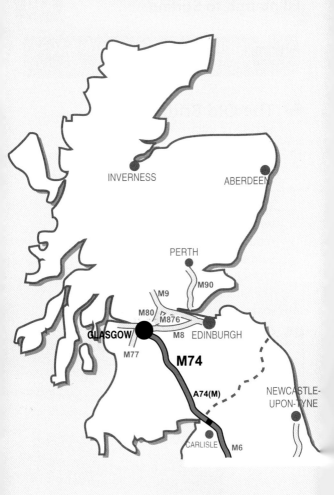

INVERNESS

ABERDEEN

PERTH

M90

M9

M80

M876

GLASGOW

M8 EDINBURGH

M77

M74

A74(M)

NEWCASTLE-
UPON-TYNE

CARLISLE   M6

M74/A74(M)

Glasgow to Carlisle

A74 (M)

Junctions   4 to 24

Within the last few years the A74 has been
rebuilt to motorway standards.
North of junction 13 it is the M74, and south to
the Border it is the A74(M).
There is nothing we could find south of
Glasgow, but the town of Moffat off Junction
15 is interesting and has a variety of places to
eat and sleep.

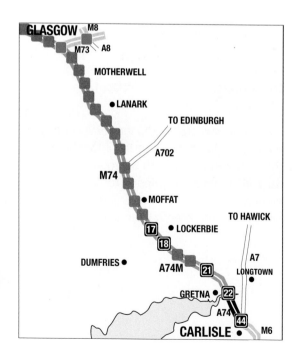

17 Lockerbie B7078
Dumfries (A709)

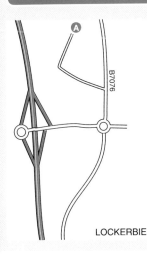

B7076

LOCKERBIE

An easy junction. You can see the hotel as soon as you get off the motorway.

Places of interest
Lochmaben Castle (HS) - 2m
Rammerscales (HHA) - 3m

Ⓐ Dryfesdale Hotel
Nr Lockerbie
☎ 01576 202 427
Last orders: 2.00pm and 9.00pm.
££ 🛏 🍷

The house was built in the late 17th century as the Manse, but was converted into a hotel in the early 1900s. It has 16 bedrooms, a restaurant and a bar catering for lunches and dinners. Dogs are welcomed. Facilities for the disabled. It has recently changed hands.

17&18 Lockerbie B723 Dumfries (A709)

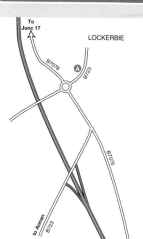

Another restricted junction, so for those driving north you have to rejoin at Junction 17 and vice versa.

A Somerton House Hotel and Resturant

Lockerbie

☎ 01576 202 583

Last orders: 2.00pm and 9.00pm every day

££ 🍴 🍷

A privately owned hotel with a friendly atmosphere.
It has 11 well furnished bedrooms, a restaurant, conservatory and bars as well as a car park and garden.
Dogs and children welcome.

21&22 Annan
Canonbie B6357

Not easy to follow, but at least you can get on and off from both directions.

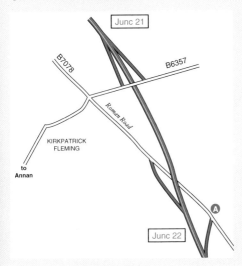

Ⓐ The Mill
Grahamshill
☎ 01461 800 344
Last orders: 8.45pm. Dinners only.
££ 🛏

The Mill started life as a farmhouse in 1740 and was converted into a hotel and restaurant in the 1990s. It has 27 bedrooms, restaurant and a bar, all on one level so it is suitable for the disabled. Children and dogs are welcome.

25 Longton A6071
Gretna Green B7076

This is really for those coming from the south
and even then it is a detour to regain the
motorway. Those driving down from the north
should drive through Gretna Green and follow
the B6076.

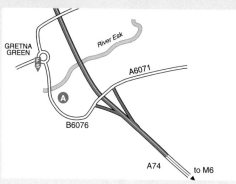

Ⓐ The Gretna Chase Hotel
Gretna Green
☎ 01461 337 517
Last orders: 3.00pm and 9.30pm.
£££ 🛏

It was built in 1865 by the owner of the Toll
Bar over the river to house runaway couples.
They had to spend a statutory two weeks in
residence before being allowed to wed. It is
still a family run hotel with 9
bedrooms and a comfortable
restaurant and bar.
Dogs allowed
but outdoors.

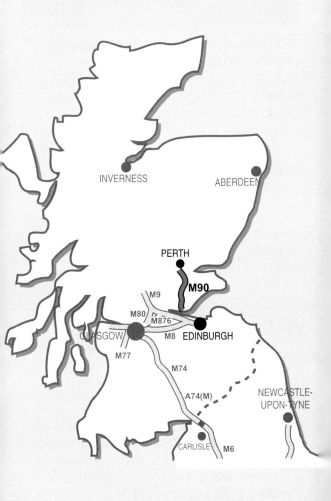

INVERNESS

ABERDEEN

PERTH

M90

M9

M80

M876

M8

GLASGOW

EDINBURGH

M77

M74

A74(M)

NEWCASTLE-
UPON-TYNE

CARLISLE

M6

M90

Edinburgh to Perth

An interesting motorway as you pass Loch Leven, where Mary Queen of Scots was imprisoned, with the Lomond Hills beyond. Further on the motorway climbs gently up to Glenfarg and then drops down to cross the Bridge of Earn. Beyond Moncrieffe Hill are the outskirts of Perth and to the north can be seen the distant outline of the Highlands.

There are castles such as Huntingtower and Elcho to be seen and to the east is Abernethy where William the Conqueror took the personal submission of the Scottish king Malcolm Canmore in 1072.

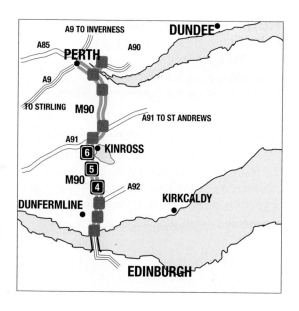

> **4**   Kelty A909
> Dollar B914

You can see the Butterchurn from the motorway when coming from the south.

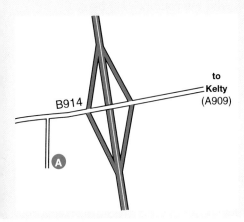

Ⓐ Kathellan Fine Food
Kelty.
☎ 01383 830 169.
Last orders; From 9.00am to 9.00pm.
High Teas between 4.30pm and 6.00pm.
£££

Once a farm, which then started a sideline in teas and coffees. Previously known as the Butterchurcn it has recently changed hands and now has a comfortable restaurant. Theatre gift and crafts shops with 50 different types of cheese and meat, supporting small suppliers.

5 Crook of Devon B9097
Glenrothes

The hotel which is about two miles away, seems further than you would expect.

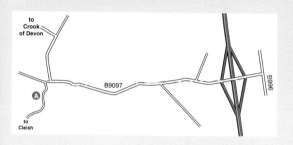

A **Nivingston House Hotel** ✳
Cleish
☎ 01577 850 216
Last orders: 2.00pm and 9.00pm.
£££ 🛏 🍷

A family owned hotel set in 12 acres of garden at the foot of the Cleish Hills. The Victorian addition masks the original building of 1725. It has 9 bedrooms with a restaurant, bar and a lounge. Morning coffee and teas. Children and dogs permitted.

6 Kinross A977

The private road to the Grouse and Claret is
opposite the Esso Filling Station. If it is full,
there are at least four good hotels in Kinross.

Places of Interest: *Loch Leven Castle.(HS) - 2m
Kinross House Garden (HHA) - 1m*

 # The Grouse and Claret

Heatheryford
☎ 01577 864 212
Last orders; From 2.00pm to 9.00pm.
No evening meals on Sundays. Closed
Mondays.
££

A surprisingly peaceful spot, with a large
garden looking onto a small loch. An
imaginative menu, with a hint of the East, in a
comfortable restaurant with a bar.
Outside seating.
Dogs and children
welcome.
Parking for
caravans and
horseboxes.

Notes

Notes

Alphabetical Index

Alphabetical Index

Alphabetical Index

Alphabetical Index

Alphabetical Index

Alphabetical Index

Alphabetical Index

Alphabetical Index

SCOTLAND

Index by Motorways

ENGLAND & WALES

Index by Motorways

Index by Motorways

Index by Motorways

Index by Motorways

Index by Motorways

SCOTLAND

READERS' RESPONSE

If you think that we have missed any places which should be included or that circumstances have altered, such as a change of ownership, which would mean an addition, amendment or even deletion, then please let us know using the following page(s).

If your suggestions are included in the next issue, we will send you a free copy of the new edition.

Name . . . .

Address . . . .

. . . .

Post Code . . . . .TN . . . .

I would suggest that be amended as follows:

Inclusions

Name . . . .

Motorway . . . . .Junction . . . .Location . . . .

Details . . . .

. . . .

. . . .

Amendments/Deletions

Name. . . . .

Motorway . . . . .Junction . . . .Location . . . .

Details . . . .

. . . .

. . . .

To:

Cheviot Books
Belford Hall
Belford
Northumberland
NE70 7EY
Tel: 01688 213 313

READERS' RESPONSE

If you think that we have missed any places which should be included or that circumstances have altered, such as a change of ownership, which would mean an addition, amendment or even deletion, then please let us know using the following page(s).

If your suggestions are included in the next issue, we will send you a free copy of the new edition.

Name . . . .

Address . . . .

. . . .

Post Code . . . . .TN . . . .

I would suggest that be amended as follows:

Inclusions

Name . . . .

Motorway . . . . .Junction . . . .Location . . . .

Details . . . .

. . . .

. . . .

Amendments/Deletions

Name. . . . .

Motorway . . . . .Junction . . . .Location . . . .

Details . . . .

. . . .

. . . .

To:

Cheviot Books
Belford Hall
Belford
Northumberland
NE70 7EY
Tel: 01688 213 313

READERS' RESPONSE

If you think that we have missed any places which should be included or that circumstances have altered, such as a change of ownership, which would mean an addition, amendment or even deletion, then please let us know using the following page(s).

If your suggestions are included in the next issue, we will send you a free copy of the new edition.

Name . . . .

Address . . . .

. . . .

Post Code . . . . .TN . . . .

I would suggest that be amended as follows:

Inclusions

Name . . . .

Motorway . . . . .Junction . . . .Location . . . .

Details . . . .

. . . .

. . . .

Amendments/Deletions

Name. . . . .

Motorway . . . . .Junction . . . .Location . . . .

Details . . . .

. . . .

. . . .

To:

Cheviot Books
Belford Hall
Belford
Northumberland
NE70 7EY
Tel: 01688 213 313

Reader's Purchase Order Form

In the event that you are unable to obtain a copy of "Breaks near the Motorways" on-line or from your local bookshop please complete the details below.

Please send me .... copy/s of A Break from the Motorways @ £9.95 plus £1 postage & packing per copy

I enclose a cheque for £............ made payable to Cheviot Books

Name: ....

Address: ....

....

....

Post Code: .... ☎: ....

Special Instructions:

....

....

....

To:

Cheviot Books
Belford Hall
Belford
Northumberland
NE70 7EY
Tel: 01688 213 313